DrawPlus X6
Resource Guide

Contacting Serif

Contacting Serif Support

On the web

Support	http://www.serif.com/support

Additional Serif information

Serif website	http://www.serif.com
You[Tube] YouTube	http://youtube.com/serifsoftware

Main office

Address	The Software Centre, PO Box 2000, Nottingham, NG11 7GW, UK
Phone	(0115) 914 2000
Phone (Registration)	(0800) 376 1989
	+44 800 376 1989
	800-794-6876 (US, Canada)
Phone (Sales)	(0800) 376 7070
	+44 800 376 7070
	800-489-6703 (US, Canada)
Customer Service	0845 345 6770
	800-489-6720 (US, Canada)
Fax	(0115) 914 2020

Credits

This Resource Guide, and the software described in it, is furnished under an end user License Agreement, which is included with the product. The agreement specifies the permitted and prohibited uses.

Trademarks

Serif is a registered trademark of Serif (Europe) Ltd.

DrawPlus is a registered trademark of Serif (Europe) Ltd.

All Serif product names are trademarks of Serif (Europe) Ltd.

Microsoft, Windows, and the Windows logo are registered trademarks of Microsoft Corporation. All other trademarks acknowledged.

Windows Vista and the Windows Vista Start button are trademarks or registered trademarks of Microsoft Corporation in the United States and/or other countries.

Adobe Flash is a registered trademark of Adobe Systems Incorporated in the United States and/or other countries.

Wacom, the logo and Intuos are trademarks or registered trademarks of the Wacom Company, Ltd.

Copyrights

Digital Images © 2008 Hemera Technologies Inc. All Rights Reserved.

Digital Images © 2008 Jupiterimages Corporation, All Rights Reserved.

Digital Images © 2008 Jupiterimages France SAS, All Rights Reserved.

Bitstream Font content © 1981-2005 Bitstream Inc. All rights reserved.

This application was developed using LEADTOOLS, copyright © 1991-2007 LEAD Technologies, Inc. ALL Rights Reserved.

Panose Typeface Matching System © 1991, 1992, 1995-1997 Hewlett-Packard Corporation.

The Sentry Spelling-Checker Engine © 2000 Wintertree Software Inc.

PANTONE® Colors displayed in the software application or in the user documentation may not match PANTONE-identified standards. Consult current PANTONE Color Publications for accurate color. PANTONE® and other Pantone trademarks are the property of Pantone LLC. ©Pantone LLC, 2012.

Pantone LCC is the copyright owner of color data and/or software which are licensed to Serif (Europe) Ltd. to distribute for use only in combination with DrawPlus. PANTONE Color Data and/or Software shall not be copied onto another disk or into memory unless as part of the execution of DrawPlus.

FontForge © 2000,2001,2002,2003,2004,2005,2006,2007,2008 by George Williams.

Portions of this software are copyright © 2008 The FreeType Project (www.freetype.org). All rights reserved.

Anti-Grain Geometry - Version 2.4 © 2002-2005 Maxim Shemanarev (McSeem)

TrueType font samples from Serif FontPacks © Serif (Europe) Ltd.

© 2013 Serif (Europe) Ltd. All rights reserved. No part of this Resource Guide may be reproduced in any form without the express written permission of Serif (Europe) Ltd.

Serif DrawPlus X6 © 1991-2013 Serif (Europe) Ltd. All rights reserved.

Companies and names used in samples are fictitious.

Introduction

This Resource Guide brings together a range of tutorials which cover techniques for using the fundamental tools in DrawPlus X6. The Resource Guide concludes with a creative showcase to provide inspiration for your drawing and illustration projects.

1: Drawing

This chapter provides illustration exercises which help you use the variety of drawing tools available in DrawPlus, from predesigned content to QuickShapes to professional line and vector drawings.

2: Colour and Opacity

The tutorials in this chapter help you work with a range of colour and opacity tools. These exercises add depth to illustrations using solid, gradient and mesh fills, plus transparency effects.

3: Typography

Why not get creative with text? The tutorials in this chapter help you work with text within DrawPlus and show how to customize and embellish it to create fantastic typographical effects.

4: Creative Showcase

Be inspired by the work in this chapter! The examples were created using stencils, brushes, gallery content, and graphic styles from the Stencils, Brushes, Gallery, and Styles tabs, respectively. A selection of samples provided with DrawPlus are also shown. Instructions on accessing these areas of DrawPlus are included.

Working with tutorials

Throughout the Resource Guide, you'll be prompted to access resource files. These files have been provided to get you started or to help focus on a key learning point.

Accessing the resource files

All resource files are free and are accessible via the Internet at the following location:

http://go.serif.com/resources/DPX6

Once you've clicked on a file, you can either open or save it. We recommend you save the file to your desktop or a named folder on your computer.

Useful icons

Here is a quick guide to the icons you'll find useful along the way.

 When you see this icon, there are project files and/or images available for download that will help you complete the tutorial.

 Don't forget to save your work! We'll remind you along the way with these helpful save points.

 These give an estimate of how long a tutorial will take to complete.

 For guidance, tutorials are graded between 1 (beginner) - 5 (advanced).

 This is a note. Notes provide useful information about the program or a particular technique.

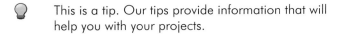 This is a tip. Our tips provide information that will help you with your projects.

⚠ This is a warning! We don't want to make you panic but when you see this icon, you need to pay attention to the steps as they will be particularly important.

Further Resources

There are a range of further resources available to help you get the most from DrawPlus.

- **Online video tutorials**
  These videos guide you through a range of techniques for using the tools available in DrawPlus.
  Available from the DrawPlus Startup Wizard's **Learn** section.

- **Comprehensive DrawPlus Help**
  The DrawPlus Help provides information and instructions on using all the tools, features, and settings within DrawPlus.
  Available via the **Help** menu (or press the **F1** key).

- **How To tab**
  The How To tab provides basic information about DrawPlus tools and features, and includes step-by-step instructions and automated assistance.
  Available within DrawPlus (displayed on the left-hand side by default).

Exploring DrawPlus X6

(A) Standard toolbar, (B) How To & Properties tabs, (C) Drawing toolbar, (D) Pasteboard, (E) Page Locator, (F) Hintline toolbar, (G) Pages tab, (H) View controls, (I) Pressure, Navigator, & View tabs (collapsed), (J) Arrange, Transform, & Align tabs, (K) Page area, (L) Styles, Brushes, Layers, & Gallery tabs, (M) Colour, Swatch, Transparency, Line & Stencils tabs, (N) Context toolbar.

The DrawPlus workspace

The DrawPlus studio workspace consists of:

- A page area i.e., where you draw your masterpiece!

- A surrounding pasteboard area (D), where you can keep elements that are being prepared or waiting to be positioned on the page area. In the example above, we have used this to place our colour reference swatches. This is not displayed when the page is exported.

- Horizontal and vertical **toolbars** and **tabs,** used to access DrawPlus commands and tools.

 Move the mouse pointer around the screen and you'll see popup **tooltips** that identify toolbar buttons and flyouts.

 Right-click any object or page region to bring up a **context menu** of functions.

Contents

Creative Showcase... 215

Drawing

At the heart of DrawPlus lies the ability to create stunning drawings and illustrations. In this section, we'll explore the tools within DrawPlus which allow you to design using lines, shapes, gallery content and brushes. Sounds complicated but really it's very straightforward!

The Gallery

 15-20 min

The DrawPlus **Gallery** tab provides you with a wealth of resources to help you create a multitude of different documents, charts, and drawings. The Gallery may not contain the exact object that you need, but it may contain something similar that you can use as a template to quickly create the object that you want. You can also add your own creations so that you can easily reuse them in future projects.

By the end of this tutorial you will be able to:

• Add Gallery objects to the page.

• Edit Gallery objects.

• Add your own creations to the Gallery.

Let's begin...

* In the Startup Wizard, choose **Start New Drawing**, select a page size of your choice and click **OK**.

Adding Galley objects

We'll start by adding a Gallery object to your page.

To add a Gallery object to the page:

1. On the **Gallery** tab, in the category drop-down list, expand the **Clipart** category then click **Animals**.

    This sub-category is also displayed by default.

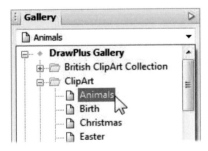

2. On the **Drawing** toolbar, from the Pointer Tool flyout, select the
   ↖ **Pointer Tool** and then drag the **Crab** graphic from the
   Gallery tab to the page.

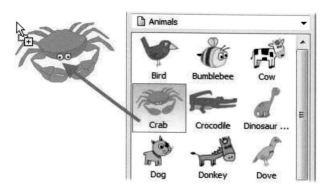

The object is placed on release.

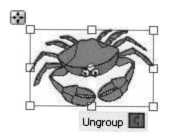

 Most of the Gallery objects are **Grouped** objects. Any changes you apply to
a group affect the whole group (including changes to fills and lines). To
make any changes to individual elements, you'll first need to 🔲 **Ungroup**
the Gallery object.

🔺 **Save now!** Click **File** > **Save As** and choose a new name for
your file.

Editing Galley objects

Any object in the Gallery can be modified to suit your own design. There are several ways of doing this and we can't hope to cover them all. However, as the basic steps are always the same, we'll give you a few ideas to get you started—resizing, changing colour, and changing text.

To resize a Gallery object:

1.   With the ⬉ **Pointer Tool**, click the **Crab** to select it.

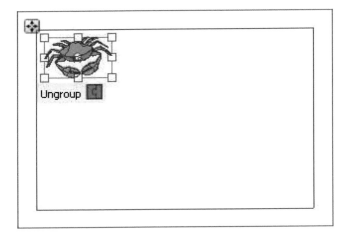

2.   Click and drag a corner handle to make the image bigger.

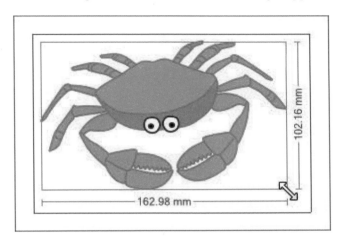

 If you use a corner handle to resize a grouped object, the aspect ratio is maintained automatically. If you press and hold **Ctrl** while resizing, the centre point of the object will remain 'locked' to the page—especially useful when resizing an object in place.

 Don't forget to save your work!

To change the colour of a Gallery object:

1.   On the **Gallery** tab, in the category drop-down list, expand the **Clipart** category then click **Party**.

2.   Using the **↖ Pointer Tool**, drag the **Balloon** from the **Gallery** tab to the page.

3. Click 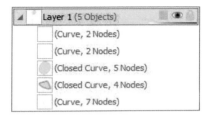 Ungroup. On the **Layers** tab, you'll see that the balloon is made up of five objects.

Layer 1 (5 Objects)
(Curve, 2 Nodes)
(Curve, 2 Nodes)
(Closed Curve, 5 Nodes)
(Closed Curve, 4 Nodes)
(Curve, 7 Nodes)

4. On the **Layers** tab, click the **Closed Curve, 5 Nodes** object. The main part of the balloon is selected.

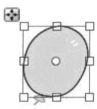

5. On the **Swatch** tab, apply a bright red **Fill** and a darker red **Line**.

 For more information on using the Swatch tab, see *Solid Fills* on p. 129.

6. To format the end of the balloon, on the **Standard** toolbar, click **Format Painter**.

7.   With the cursor, click the end of the balloon.

The format is copied from the large shape to the small shape.

8.   Finally, select all of the objects again and click ■ **Group**.

> 💡 We always recommend that you Group the objects together again after making changes to individual elements as this helps to structure a large drawing.

To change the text in a Gallery object:

1. On the **Gallery** tab, in the category drop-down list, select the **Home** category and **Fun & Crafts** sub-category then click **Scrapbooking**.

2. Using the ↖ **Pointer Tool**, drag the yellow **Price** object from the **Gallery** tab to the page.

3. On the **Hintline** toolbar, click ◉ **Solo Mode** (a **Solo Mode** window opens) and then select the text object on the page.

4. On the **Drawing** toolbar, from the Text Tool flyout, select the A Artistic Text Tool.

   A cursor appears in the text object ready for you to edit the text.

5. Type in a new price and then, in the **Solo Mode** window, click ⤢ **Unsolo** to resume normal editing.

💡 Solo mode is a great way of editing objects within a complex drawing.

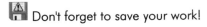 Don't forget to save your work!

Storing your own content in the Gallery

One of the most useful things about the DrawPlus Gallery is the ability to add your own creations. This way, they are available for use in any future project. What's more, it's really easy to do!

To add an object to the Gallery:

1. On the **Gallery** tab, in the category drop-down list, expand the **My Designs** category.

2. Using the ⬉ **Pointer Tool**, drag your red balloon from the page to the **Gallery** tab.

3. In the **Add Design** dialog, type a name for your object and click OK.

    A copy of the object is added to the **Gallery** tab.

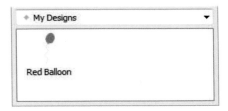

That's it! Now you know how to use the Gallery tab, you can
quickly build up some fantastic designs! Search *Using the Gallery*
in DrawPlus Help for further information.

There's so much more you can do!

Below is an example of what else you can do...

Chemistry equipment

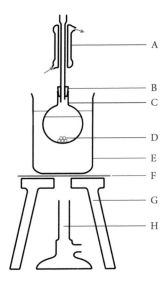

This diagram was created using objects in **School** > **Sciences** >
Chemistry > **Laboratory Equipment** (marked in black). The other
lines were created using the Straight Line Tool, the red circles
were created from Quick Ellipses, and the text was added using
the Artistic Text Tool.

Basic QuickShapes

 10-15 min

In this tutorial we are going to get creative with QuickShapes! DrawPlus has a lot of useful QuickShapes, and with a little imagination, they can be used to create a lot more than a few simple shapes on the page.

By the end of this tutorial you will be able to:

- Add QuickShapes to a page.

- Use the Node tool to edit QuickShapes.

 Go to **http://go.serif.com/resources/DPX6** to download the following resource file(s):

⬇ **quickshapes.dpp**

Let's begin...

1.   On the **Standard** toolbar, click **Open**.

2.   Locate **QuickShapes.dpp** and click **Open**.

The drawing opens on the first page displaying a single line.

> The line was created in advance using the **Pen Tool**, so you could
> concentrate on the main learning objective—using QuickShapes. See
> *Penning a Sketch* on p. 65 and search *Drawing lines and shapes* in DrawPlus
> Help for more information on creating lines.

Drawing a flower

We'll begin by drawing the flower's head.

To create the flower head:

1.   On the **Drawing** toolbar, on the QuickShapes flyout, click the
     ❀ **Quick Petal**. Press and hold the **Shift** key while dragging on
     your page to draw the flower.

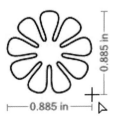

The **Shift** key is a really useful modifier key as it constrains the shape's proportions. When drawing QuickShapes, it keeps the width and the height equal. Another useful modifier key is **Ctrl**. When pressed, a QuickShape will resize from the centre instead of the corner of the bounding box. Try it and see for yourself!

2. On the **Line** tab, change the line width to 1.5 pt.

If necessary, re-position the flower head so it is at the top of the curved line.

3. On the **Drawing** toolbar, click the 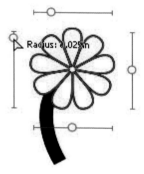 Node Tool and drag the leftmost node upwards until the petals just touch.

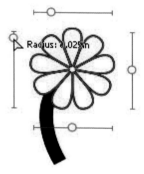

4.   On the **Drawing** toolbar, in the QuickShapes flyout, click the
     ⬤ **Quick Ellipse**. Press and hold the **Shift** key while dragging on
     your page to draw the centre of your flower. Re-position it as
     needed.

Now for the leaves...

To create the leaves:

1.   On the **Drawing** toolbar, in the QuickShapes flyout, click the
     ♡ **Quick Heart**. Click and drag on the page to draw the heart.

2. Drag the left node down to the bottom.

3. Position the cursor just outside a corner handle on the boundary box then click and drag to rotate the leaves slightly to complete the effect.

That's it! You've drawn a flower using a few QuickShapes.

Save now! Click **File > Save As** and choose a new name for your file.

There's so much more you can do!

Below are some examples of what else you can do...

Experiment with Quick Petals

Experiment by adjusting the nodes on the Quick Petal to see what other flower shapes you can create.

Colour the flower

You can apply solid or gradient colours to each element of your flower. See *Solid Fills* (p. 129) and *Gradient Fills* (p. 141) for more information.

Off Canvas

 10 min

In the tutorial *Basic QuickShapes* (p. 13), we show that, with a little imagination, QuickShapes can be used to create a variety of drawings directly on the page. We'll take QuickShapes in another direction! By thinking outside the box (or off canvas) you can expand your creative possibilities!

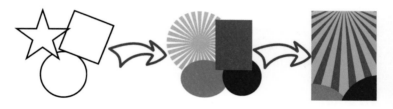

By the end of this tutorial you will be able to:

• Set a zoom level and work on the pasteboard.

• Add QuickShapes to the workspace.

• View a design in Dynamic Preview mode.

Let's begin...

- In the Startup Wizard, choose **Start New Drawing**, select a page size of your choice and click **OK**.

To give this tutorial a focus, we're going to create a poster which could be used to advertise a summer festival.

Zooming out

We're going to be working off canvas to achieve our creative outcome. It is therefore useful to zoom out so we can see a large section of the surrounding pasteboard.

To zoom out:

1. From the **View** menu, select **Zoom**.

2. In the **Edit Zoom** dialog, select **25%** and click **OK**.

Now we can see a lot of the grey pasteboard, let's add some QuickShapes to create our poster background.

Adding QuickShapes

Summer festival posters frequently feature a starburst and rolling green hills. By working off canvas we can hide parts of the shapes to create our design.

To add a starburst design:

1. On the **Drawing** toolbar, from the QuickShapes flyout, click the ☆ Quick Star.

2. Click and drag in your workspace to create a large star—hold the **Shift** key to constrain its proportions.

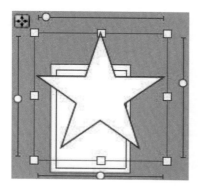

3. On the context toolbar:

    • Set the **Points** to **30**.

    • Set the **Minor Radius** to **0%**.

- Set the **Inner Radius** to 100%.

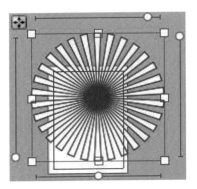

4. Click and drag the shape's 🔀 move button to position the star so the centre is just off the top of the page and, on the **Align** tab, click ⬓ **Centre Horizontally**.

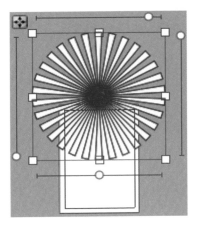

5.   Click and drag from a corner handle to resize the star so the bottom fills the entire page—hold the **Shift** and **Ctrl** keys to constrain the star and resize from its centre.

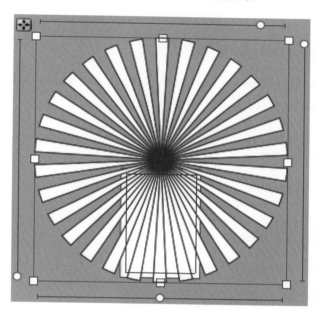

The starburst design is now complete, but might be hard to envisage at the moment. We'll recolour the shape next.

Save now! Click **File > Save As** and choose a new name for your file.

Recolour a shape

Let's change the object's colour to a bold yellow and then view it in Dynamic Preview mode so we can see the design clearly.

To apply a colour fill:

1. With the star selected, from the **Swatch** tab, click to select the **Line** swatch, e.g. .

2. Click the ▼ **Palettes** drop-down arrow and select a palette from the list.

3. From the palette, click to select an orange swatch.

4. Click to select the **Fill** swatch, e.g. , and select the same orange swatch again.

    The colour is applied to the star's line and fill.

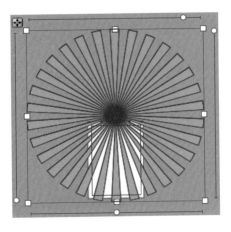

Now to view the page without any distractions...

To view a page in Dynamic Preview mode:

1. On the **Drawing** toolbar, click the 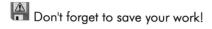 **Pointer Tool** and click anywhere in the workspace to deselect the shape.

2. On the **Hintline** toolbar, click **Dynamic Preview**.

The page is displayed with all areas outside the canvas hidden.

Search *Dynamic Preview* in DrawPlus Help for more information.

 Don't forget to save your work!

Adding to the design

Now we can continue designing our poster with the knowledge of how working off canvas can affect our design.

First let's return to normal design mode...

To exit Dynamic Preview mode:

• On the **Hintline** toolbar, click 🔊 ▾ Dynamic Preview.

Now we'll add some rolling hills...

To add to the design:

1. On the **Drawing** toolbar, from the QuickShapes flyout, click the ⬤ Quick Ellipse.

2. Click and drag in your workspace to create a large ellipse.

3. Position the shape to the bottom left of your design, so only the top right lies over the page.

4.   Recolour the ellipse with green.

5.   Add a second ellipse, position it to the bottom right and apply a different colour green.

In Dynamic Preview mode you can see the ellipses now resemble hills!

Finally, to complete the summer feel, we'll add a beautiful blue sky.

To add a blue sky:

1. On the **Drawing** toolbar, from the QuickShapes flyout, click the 🔲 **Quick Rectangle**.

2. Click and drag a rectangle which encompasses the entire page and then apply a blue colour.

3. On the **Standard** toolbar, click ⬛ **Send to Back**.

That's it! The basic summer poster design is complete.

Now, when you print or export it all the elements outside the page (canvas) are ignored, giving a poster as illustrated below.

Search *Printing basics* and *Exporting objects and drawings* in DrawPlus Help for more details.

Don't forget to save your work!

Expand the design and add artistic and shape text:

You can add graphics to your basic poster design to give an indication of the type of festival you are advertising. All the graphics added in the above example were taken from the Vectors category on the Gallery tab.

Text can be quickly and easily added to your design using artistic and frame text. See *Artistic, Shape and Frame Text* on p. 179 for full details.

See *The Gallery* on p. 3 and search *Using the Gallery* in DrawPlus Help for more information.

 The coloured crowd was created by combining several people graphics and then clipping a copy of the starburst and sky design to the crowd graphic. To learn these techniques see *Building a Dragon with Shapes* (p. 41) and *Transforming a Folding Fan* (p. 51).

Modifying Shapes

 5-10 min

In this tutorial we are going to draw several cartoons by using and modifying QuickShapes! If you haven't done so already, you might find it easier to complete *Basic QuickShapes* on p. 13 first.

By the end of this tutorial you will be able to:

* Use Convert to Curves to create a new shape from a QuickShape.

* Use the Node tool to transform shapes and lines.

* Copy shapes.

If you look at the opening example, you'll notice that the cartoons all start from a basic pear shape. To create this, we will modify a Quick Ellipse by converting it to curves and then using the Node Tool.

Let's begin...

*   In the Startup Wizard, choose **Start New Drawing**, select a
    page size of your choice and click **OK**.

Converting an object to curves

If you want to dramatically modify your QuickShape, you'll need
to 'convert it to curves'. This basically means that it stops being a
QuickShape and instead becomes an object made up of a line
with curved segments.

Although we are using a QuickShape in this tutorial, you can also convert
text and other objects to curves in the same way. This is especially useful if
you want to share artwork that uses an unusual font as it converts the text to
shaped objects. This means that it will look the same, but will no longer be
editable text, so the font isn't needed any more. See *Customizing Artistic Text*
on p. 195 for more information.

To convert a shape to curves:

1. On the **Drawing** toolbar, on the QuickShapes flyout, click the
    ⬤ **Quick Ellipse** and drag on the page to create an ellipse.

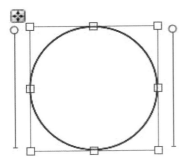

2. On the **Drawing** toolbar, click the ▷ **Node Tool**.

With the shape selected, on the **Arrange** tab, click ○ **Convert to Curves**. You'll see four nodes appear on the ellipse's edge and the cursor changes to ▷.

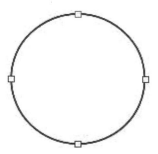

 Save now! Click **File** > **Save As** and choose a new name for your file.

Adjusting nodes

Converting a shape to curves allows you to edit it using the Node Tool and the Curves context toolbar. We'll do this next.

> ✎ Lines and shapes consist of curve segments, nodes and control handles.
>
> When you click on a node, the ⌒⌒⌒⌒⌒ **node type** buttons become available for selection from the context toolbar. The behaviour of the control handles, and the curvature of the segments on either side of a node, depend on whether the node is sharp, smooth, symmetric, or smart. We can change the node type at any time.
>
> (Search *Changing nodes and line segments* in DrawPlus Help and the **How To** tab for more information.)

To adjust a line with the Node Tool:

1. With the 🖑 cursor, drag the topmost node upwards to create an egg shape.

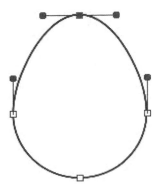

2. Move the cursor over the line at the point where you want to add a node.

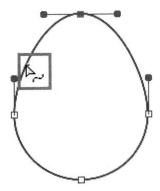

When the cursor changes to ⮥ click once to add a node.

3. On the context toolbar, click ⟋ **Sharp corner** to change the node type.

4. With the ⮥ cursor, drag the node in to decrease the width of the upper segment.

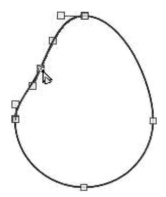

5. Drag the node handle upwards to change the shape of the line segment.

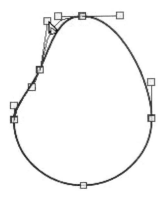

The other segment doesn't change because we changed the node type to a sharp corner.

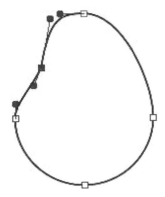

6. Repeat the add and adjust process for the other side of the shape so that it looks symmetrical.

7. To change the shape of the base slightly, select the node on the widest part, and with the 🔈 cursor, drag the handle downwards. Repeat for the opposite side.

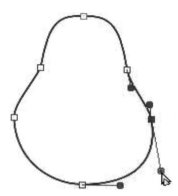

8. Finally to round the base off a little, select the bottom node and on the context toolbar, click ⌒ **Symmetric corner**.

9. Drag the node handle inwards.

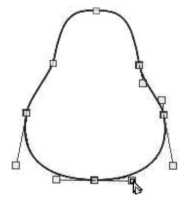

Notice that both handles move in at the same time.

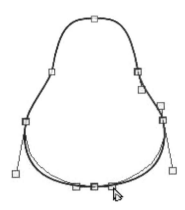

That's it! Your pear shape should now be complete.

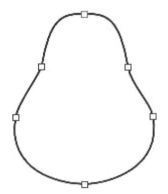

You may wish to copy it to the Gallery tab to use in other DrawPlus projects. Search *Using the Gallery* in DrawPlus Help for more details.

 Now you've learned how to edit lines with the node tool, this technique can be applied whenever you need to adjust a line.

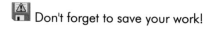 Don't forget to save your work!

Using your modified shape

Now we have the basic modified shape, let's take a brief look at how we can use it.

Penguin

The body of the penguin uses a copy of the pear shape. The wings, eyes and feet are basic QuickShapes:

- The wings are made from a single **Quick Polygon** which we copied and flipped using ⚑ **Flip Horizontal** on the **Arrange** tab.

- The eyes are created from two **Quick Ellipses**. The 'pupil' is created by adjusting the nodes on the ellipse to create the shine. The right eye is a copy of the left.

 Save time and effort by copying elements that you have already created! You can always flip or rotate the copy if necessary.

Cat and Mouse

Shapes used:

- Our modified ellipse or 'Pear' (black)

- Quick Ellipse (red)

- Quick Badge (purple)

- Quick Tear (turquoise)

The whiskers were drawn using the 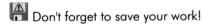 **Straight Line Tool** (Pen Tool flyout).

 🖿 🖿 🖿 🖿 You can re-arrange the **Z-order** of your objects using the tools—**Bring to Front, Forward One, Back One** and **Send to Back**—on the **Arrange** tab. Search *Ordering Objects* in DrawPlus Help for more information.

💾 Don't forget to save your work!

Building a Dragon with Shapes

 15-20 min

In this tutorial we are going to combine a variety of QuickShapes to build a dragon! Even if you don't consider yourself artistic in nature, you'll be amazed at what you can create by combining the QuickShapes on offer using the Shape Builder Tool.

 We'll not go into details here on how to add and modify QuickShapes as this is covered in *Basic QuickShapes* on p. 13.

By the end of this tutorial you will be able to:

- Combine (add) shapes together using the Shape Builder Tool.

- Subtract intersecting shapes using the Shape Builder Tool.

- Adding and subtracting with the Arrange tab.

Let's begin...

* In the Startup Wizard, choose **Start New Drawing**, select a page size of your choice and click **OK**.

Combining (Adding) shapes together

We'll begin by drawing the head of the dragon to show you how ellipses can be used to create a irregular but smooth-curved shape.

To combine shapes:

1. On the **Drawing** toolbar, on the QuickShapes flyout, click the
   ○ Quick Ellipse.

2. Click and drag on your page to draw an ellipse.

3. Hover the cursor just outside a corner handle and click and drag to rotate the ellipse so the right side is slightly lower than the left.

4. Add two smaller ellipses to the page and then partially overlay them with the first ellipse as illustrated below.

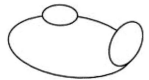

These will form the basis of a snout and eye.

5. On the **Drawing** toolbar, click the Shape Builder Tool.

6. Position your cursor over the first, largest ellipse (it will show as highlighted), then click and drag to position your cursor over a non-overlapping section of one of the other ellipses.

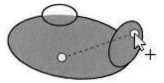

7. Release the mouse button to finish combining the ellipses.

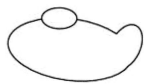

8.   Repeat steps 6 and 7 to combine this new shape with the third ellipse.

Now you have the hang of combining shapes using the Shape Builder Tool, why not combine some Quick Moon shapes with your irregular head shape to add horns?

Our dragon's head is taking shape but doesn't quite look like a head yet. We can give the irregular shape character by removing parts! We'll show you this next...

Save now! Click **File > Save As** and choose a new name for your file.

Subtracting shapes

The Shape Builder Tool allows you to combine shapes together intuitively on the page, however, it has other additional properties, including subtracting intersecting shapes!

To subtract shapes:

1. On the **Drawing** toolbar, on the QuickShapes flyout, click the Quick Tear.

2. Click and drag on your page to draw a very small tear.

3. Rotate the tear and position it on the head's snout section. The tear will form a nostril!

4. Add a second tear (with the tail position set to 50%) and rotate and position it to form the eye.

5. On the **Drawing** toolbar, click the Shape Builder Tool.

6. Position your cursor over the first tear (it will show as highlighted) and hold down the **Alt** key—the cursor will change to show a subtract (-) sign.

7. Click to subtract the tear shape from the head shape.

8. Repeat steps 6 and 7 to subtract the second tear shape.

It may appear as if nothing has changed, but the illustration below shows the difference more clearly.

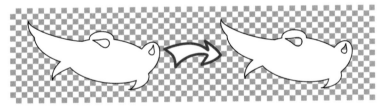

Now you have the hang of combining and subtracting shapes using the Shape Builder Tool, why not combine two Quick Ellipses and then subtract them from the head shape to form the dragon's mouth?

Our dragon's head looks excellent! If you want you can continue to build up your techniques with the Shape Builder Tool to create a neck as well.

Save now! Click **File** > **Save As** and choose a new name for your file.

More adding...

To form the shape of the neck we combined the following QuickShapes:

- One **Quick Wave**—set to 1 Peak, Top and Bottom Height of **50%**, and rotated 90°.

- One **Quick Badge**—set to Style **2**, and rotated 175°.

- Five **Quick Ellipses**.

Now you've mastered the Shape Builder Tool, we'll show you some other ways of adding and subtracting!

Save now! Click **File** > **Save As** and choose a new name for your file.

Adding and subtracting with the Arrange tab

You can also add and subtract shapes using the Arrange tab with a single click. This is an efficient way of building up irregular shapes if you can easy visualize how the shapes will join together. We'll demonstrate by building a wing for our dragon.

To combine using the Arrange tab:

1. Add two identical **Quick Waves**, set to 1 Peak, Top and Bottom Heights of **50%**, and flipped horizontally.

2. Place them together, with one above the other, and then select them both.

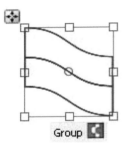

3. On the **Arrange** tab, click **Add**.

4. Add three identical **Quick Ellipses** as perfect circles and position them to cover the left and bottom sides of the wave shape as illustrated.

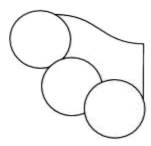

5. Select the wave shape and the three ellipses and then, on the **Arrange** tab, click 🔘 **Subtract**.

You can now place this wing behind your previously created dragon or even combine the two together!

That's it! Your dragon is complete.

🔺 Don't forget to save your work!

There's so much more you can do!

Below are some examples of what else you can do...

Explore the Styles tab

The Styles tab offers a variety of professionally designed preset styles which you can apply to your objects with a single click.

Search *Using graphic styles* in DrawPlus Help for more information.

Create other animal heads

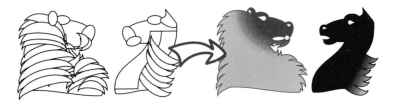

Using the techniques and QuickShapes already discussed in this tutorial, you can have a go at making any animal shape!

Transforming a Folding Fan

 15-20 min

In this tutorial we'll show you some great features of DrawPlus to create a Japanese style folded fan. You can then use the techniques learned here to expand your design repertoire.

By the end of this tutorial you will be able to:

*   Add a triangle using the Triangle Tool.

*   Apply a gradient fill.

*   Creating a basic fan shape using Transform.

*   Combining objects to apply decoration.

Let's begin...

- In the Startup Wizard, choose **Start New Drawing**, select a page size of your choice and click **OK**.

To create our basic shape, we'll transform and copy a triangle several times to simulate the slates which make up the body of a fan. So let's get started...

Adding a triangle

There are several ways of drawing a triangle. These include using the Straight Line Tool and adjusting the nodes of a Quick Polygon. However, the quickest way is to use the Triangle Tool!

To draw a triangle:

1. On the **Drawing** toolbar, from the Pen Tool flyout, click the
   △ **Triangle Tool**.

2. Click and drag on the page to create a triangle.

29.77 mm

3. On the **Transform** tab:

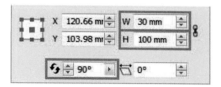

- Set the width (**W**) to **30mm** and the height (**H**) to **100mm**.

- Set the 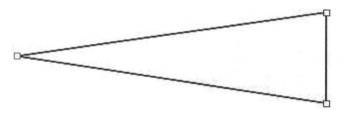 rotation angle to **90°**.

The triangle is now ready to be used to create the fan.

However, to add to the design we'll apply some colour to the triangle first.

Save now! Click **File** > **Save As** and choose a new name for your file.

Applying a colour fill

A gradient fill will give an authentic look to the fan design. This can be applied from the Swatch tab and then modified using the Fill tool.

To apply a colour fill:

1. With the triangle selected, from the **Swatch** tab, click to select the **Line** swatch, e.g. .

2. Click the **Palettes** drop-down arrow and select a palette from the list.

3. From the palette, click to select an orange swatch.

4. Click to select the **Fill** swatch, e.g. , and select the same yellow swatch again.

    The colour is applied to the triangle's line and fill.

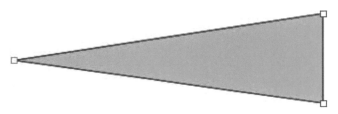

5. Click **Gradient** to display the **Automatic** gradient palette.

6. From the gradient palette, select the swatch from the third column.

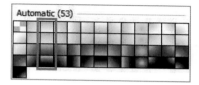

We chose the gradient from the second row.

Now we have the first blade of the fan, we need to replicate and transform it to create the basic folding fan design.

 Don't forget to save your work!

Transforming an object

Transforming provides an excellent way of copying, rotating and repositioning objects instantly. Before performing the transform operation, it is worth considering the rotation point of the object.

Currently the rotation point of the triangle is at its centre and would create a pretty pattern if rotated, but would not give the design we want...

So first we must move the triangle's rotation point.

To move a rotation point:

1. On the **Drawing** toolbar, from the Pointer Tool flyout, click the
    ↖ **Pointer Tool** and then click to select the triangle.

    The rotation point is indicated by the circle at the triangle's centre and the cursor will change to a cross if positioned over the circle.

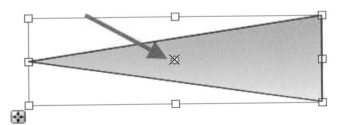

2.   Click and drag the rotation point to the left to where the triangle's lines converge.

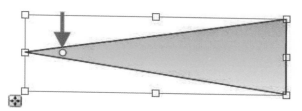

Now let's transform this triangle into a folding fan!

To copy, rotate and reposition (transform) an object:

1.   With the triangle selected, from the **Tools** menu, select **Transform**.

2.   In the **Transform** dialog:

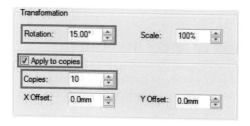

*   Set the **Rotation** to 15°.

*   Ensure the **Apply to copies** option is selected.

*   Set the **Copies** to 10.

*   Click **OK**.

Your folding fan instantly materializes.

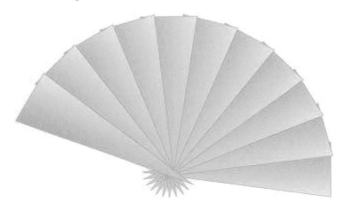

The basic folding fan shape is now complete!

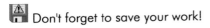 Don't forget to save your work!

Combining objects to apply decoration

The Gallery tab provides a variety of professional designed graphics which you can add to your designs quickly. We'll use this gallery content to decorate our fan.

To add gallery content:

1. From the **Gallery** tab, from the categories drop-down list, select the **Vectors** sub-category from the **Clip Art** category.

2. Click and drag **Birds03** onto the page.

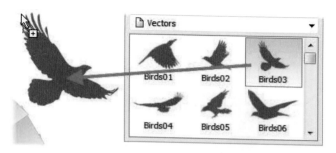

3. (Optional) With the gallery item selected, from the **Swatch** tab, select a solid fill from the **Document Palette**. We chose **Black**.

4. Click and drag the gallery item to position it within the folding fan shape (as shown below).

Once you're happy with the colour, size and position of the gallery item, proceed to the next step. This involves replicating the gallery items and then clipping each version with a single fan blade. This will give the illusion the graphic is printed on the fan!

Don't forget to save your work!

Before we replicate the gallery item, we need to determine how many copies we need. We want a copy for every fan blade the item overlaps...

In our case we need seven items in total and therefore need to duplicate the original six times.

To replicate an object using the Transform command:

1. With the gallery item selected, from the **Tools** menu, select **Transform**.

   You will notice DrawPlus has remembered the settings from your previous transform procedure!

2. In the **Transform** dialog:

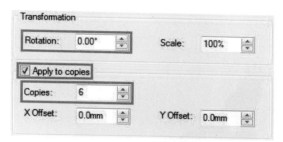

- Set the **Rotation** back to 0°.

- Ensure the **Apply to copies** option is selected.

- Set the **Copies** to number calculated (in our case, **6**).

- Click **OK**.

At first it may appear that nothing has happened. However, your selection boundary box now displays a ⊞ **Group** button (indicating multiple items are selected) and the **Layers** tab shows there are now **18 Objects**.

We now need to clip each replicated item to a single fan blade. We can do this using the Arrange tab.

Don't forget to save your work!

To clip an object:

1. Click to select the left-hand blade.

2. Hold down the **Shift** key and then click to select the gallery item which is positioned above the blade.

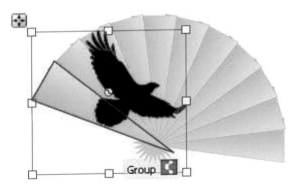

3. On the **Arrange** tab, from the 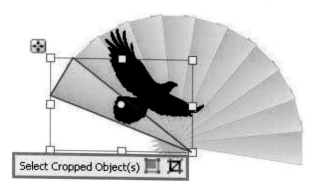 Crop/Clip flyout, select **Clip to Bottom Object**.

The options on the object boundary box will update to show that one of the gallery items has been clipped to the first fan blade.

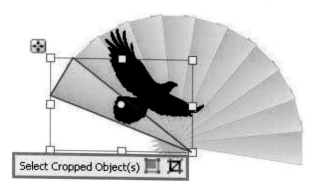

4. Click to select the next blade in the fan and then hold down the **Shift** key and click to select the gallery item which is positioned above the blade.

5. On the **Arrange** tab, simply click the Crop/Clip button—DrawPlus remembers the previously selected **Clip to Bottom Object** setting.

6. Repeat steps 4 and 5 with the other five blades and gallery items.

Your folded fan design should now resemble the example below.

That's it! The graphic now looks like it is printed on each blade separately! Your folded fan design is complete.

 Don't forget to save your work!

Why not expand on the design?

Repeat the *Combining objects to apply decoration* on p. 58 procedures to add more decorations to your fan. We also added a gradient filled Quick Ellipse at the rotation points of the blades to simulate a pin holding the blades together!

Penning a Sketch

 15-60 min

Being able to draw and edit lines is an essential technique to learn in DrawPlus. In this tutorial, we'll look at one of the most common ways to use the Pen Tool—to digitize (trace over) an original drawing.

By the end of this tutorial you will be able to:

- Import an image file.

- Trace around an object using the Pen tool.

- Adjust curves using nodes and control handles.

- Use modifier keys to increase the accuracy of drawn lines.

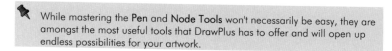

While mastering the **Pen** and **Node Tools** won't necessarily be easy, they are amongst the most useful tools that DrawPlus has to offer and will open up endless possibilities for your artwork.

Let's begin...

- In the Startup Wizard, choose **Start New Drawing**, select a page size of your choice and click **OK**.

Scanning and importing your original drawing

It's not easy to create a digital drawing from scratch. Many designers will create their drawing on paper first and then scan or photograph it. Once the drawing is in a digital format, it can be imported into DrawPlus.

This method of digitizing a drawing isn't 'cheating', it's a genuine technique that's used by artists all over the world!

So that you can follow the tutorial, we've provided an image of our skateboarding hero.

 Go to **http://go.serif.com/resources/DPX6** to download the following resource file(s):

 kit.png

 The drawing that we are working on is quite complex and will take time to trace. You don't have to trace the entire image if you don't want to! Remember, you can use any image or only trace part of our drawing, such as the head. This tutorial is filled with helpful techniques that will help you become proficient with this powerful tool.

 This method will work equally well to create a drawing from a photo.

To import the image:

1. On the **Drawing** toolbar, click **Insert Picture**.

2. In the **Insert Picture** dialog, locate the **kit.png** file, click to select it and then click **Open**.

3. Click and drag on the page to place the image so that it fills most of the page.

💡 Sometimes you might find it easier to trace your image if you reduce its opacity as this can make it easier to see your newly created lines.
   • With your image selected, on the Colour tab, click the **Fill** button.
   • Drag the **Opacity slider** to the left until the image's opacity is reduced sufficiently.

4. On the **Layers** tab, click the small padlock button to lock the layer. This will prevent the drawing from accidentally being selected when we start the line work.

Save now! Click **File** > **Save As** and choose a new name for your file.

Tracing the image

Now that we have our drawing on the page, the next thing to do is to trace an outline. Our drawing is already very 'clean', i.e., there aren't many extra sketch or construction lines. However, if you use your own drawing, it might be a very different story. When using the Pen Tool, we're aiming to create a nice, clean vector outline.

We'll create all of our lines on a new layer. This will keep things really simple and help us a lot if we decide to colour our image later on.

To create a new layer:

- On the **Layers** tab, click ✛ **Add Layer**. A new layer, Layer 2, is added above Layer 1 and is selected by default.

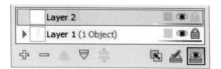

Now we're ready to start drawing. We're going to start with the head of our character so let's zoom in a little so that we can see what we're doing.

To zoom into an image:

- On the **HintLine** toolbar, click ⊕ **Zoom In** or drag the Zoom slider to the right.

The Pen Tool

There are two main tools that you could use to trace an image:

- The ✒ **Pen Tool**—used for creating extremely accurate lines and shapes.

- The ✏ **Pencil Tool**—great for drawing freeform, pressure-sensitive lines and is particularly useful if you own (or use) a pressure sensitive drawing tablet.

In this tutorial we'll be concentrating on the ✒ **Pen Tool** as you will be able to transfer many of the skills, such as node editing, between the two types of line created.

Let's get started!

To create lines using Smart Segments:

1. On the **Drawing** toolbar, from the Pen Tool flyout, click the ✒ **Pen Tool** and on the context toolbar, ensure that ⌒ **Smart segments** is selected.

 At the left of the context toolbar, notice that the ✒ **Pen Tool** has three creation modes:
- ⌒ **Smooth segments**
- ⌒ **Smart segments** (default)
- ⌒ **Line segments**

These options let you create different types of curves and joins while you are drawing your line. Search *Drawing lines and shapes* in DrawPlus Help and the How To tab for detailed information.

2. On the **Colour** tab, ensure that the **Line** colour is set to black.

3. On the context toolbar (or on the **Line** tab), ensure that the line weight is set to **1 pt**.

4. Click where the first part of the hat starts near the goggles. Then, continue clicking at each point where there is a natural change in direction. The line should begin to update to match the curve as you place the nodes. If you make a mistake, don't worry as we can easily adjust the line later.

5.   Once you have completed this first line, press the **Esc** key to tell DrawPlus that the line is complete.

At this point, we can either make adjustments to the line, or create another. Our line isn't exact, but it's pretty close, so we only need a small edit with the **Node Tool**. We can change to this temporarily by holding the **Ctrl** key.

To make quick adjustments to a line:

1.   With the 🖊 **Pen Tool** still selected, press and hold the **Ctrl** key. Notice that the cursor changes to a small arrow.

2. Move the cursor over the line, and when it changes to ⌕ click and drag the line segment into position.

3. Repeat the process for any other segments as necessary.

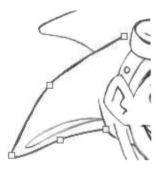

Now that the first line is completed, we're ready to continue tracing around our character. This time we'll look at a slightly different way of using the Pen Tool. Instead of simply clicking to place a node, we can click and drag to shape the line as we place it.

To create lines using Smooth Segments:

1. On the **Drawing** toolbar, click the ⌕ **Pen Tool** and on the context toolbar, ensure that ⌕ **Smooth segments** is selected.

2. Click once to place your starting node at the point where the goggles and hat join and then click and drag to place the next node. As you drag, you'll notice that the shape of the line changes. As before, follow the natural change of direction of the line.

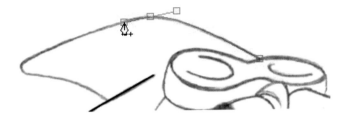

3.   On **release**, the node is placed.

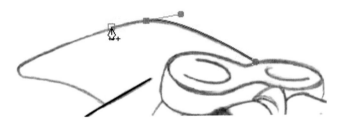

4.   Repeat the click and drag process to complete the rest of the outline.

5. At the end of the line, press **Esc** (or you can also double-click when adding the last node if you find this easier).

 Remember, if you've made a mistake while placing a node, or if you just want to change the line, you can always modify it with the ▷ **Node Tool**. See *Modifying Shapes* on p. 31, the **How To** tab and search *Editing lines and shapes* in DrawPlus Help for more details.

 Don't forget to save your work!

Using Modifiers

Modifiers are keys that temporarily change the action of a tool while they are being pressed. DrawPlus uses lots of these modifiers and they provide quick shortcuts to do certain things.

The ⬢ **Pen Tool** has some really useful modifier keys that change the type of node that is placed when you click. This allows you to more accurately place a line as it is created and hopefully reduces the amount of editing that you have to do later on (more on this in *Adjusting lines with the Node Tool* on p. 72).

One really useful modifier is the **Alt** key. This adds a sharp node to the line so that you can create corners. Let's look at this now.

To use modifiers when drawing lines:

1. On the **Drawing** toolbar, click the ☖ **Pen Tool** and on the context toolbar, ensure that ⌒ **Smooth segments** is selected.

2. Click on the sharp 'point' where the hair meets the goggles and then click and drag to create the first curved segment.

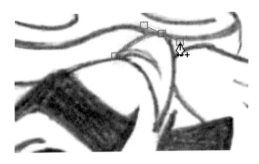

3. Next, click and drag on the point of the hair to create the next curved segment **but do not release the mouse button** yet. Once the curve is correct, press and hold the **Alt** key.

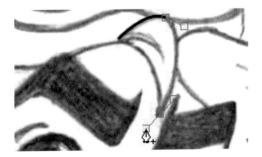

4. Still holding down the left-mouse button and **Alt**, position the control handle in the direction of your next curve segment, approximately where the next node will be.

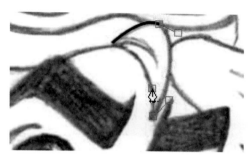

5. **Release** the **mouse** button. Finally, release the **Alt** key.

6. Click and drag to place the next node.

7. Finally, place the pointer over the green start node and click once the cursor changes to ⚬ to close the line as a shape.

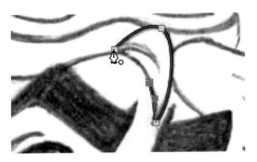

8. Your finished shape should not require any further editing and you can continue to trace the other parts of the drawing.

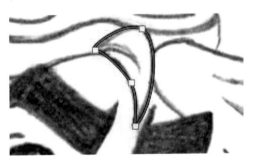

Even if you draw your lines with the help of modifier keys, there will be times when you need to have more control over editing your lines.

The ▷ **Node Tool** will give you the greatest control when you need to reshape the different segments of your line. See *Modifying Shapes* on p. 31 or search *Editing lines and shapes* in DrawPlus Help for more details.

 Don't forget to save your work!

The finishing touch

Once you've finished tracing your image, on the **Layers** tab, click ⦿ to hide **Layer 1** and the original drawing. You should end up with a neat line drawing consisting of even lines.

Congratulations on completing your drawing! By now you will have mastered the technique of drawing lines using the Pen Tool.

You can quickly transform your completed illustration to make it look hand-drawn by using the preset pressure profiles from the Pressure tab. See *Simulating Hand-Drawn Pressure* on p. 81 for more information.

 Don't forget to save your work!

There's so much more you can do!

Add colour

A line drawing can be extremely dramatic by itself, but you may wish to consider enhancing your drawing with a splash of colour. As the drawing is made up of mainly separate lines, you won't be able to do this by simply applying a fill. You will need to create coloured shapes on a layer below! See *Solid Fills* on p. 129 for more information on applying colour.

Trace a photograph

You don't have to be able to sketch to create fantastic artwork in DrawPlus! It's just as easy to trace over a photograph using the Pen Tool and awaken those artistic talents you never knew you had.

Simulating Hand-Drawn Pressure

⏱ 10-15 min ✏✏✏✏✏

In this tutorial we'll show you how you can simulate the varying thickness of a hand-drawn line, as you would find in professional pen illustrations. Simulating hand-drawn pressure can take your drawings to a whole new level.

By the end of this tutorial you will be able to:

•   Use preset Pressure profiles.

•   Adjust preset Pressure profiles.

For this tutorial, you can use any previously line drawing created in DrawPlus, however we've provided you with an illustration to work from if needed.

   Go to **http://go.serif.com/resources/DPX6** to download the following resource file(s):

🔽 kit_complete.dpp

Let's begin...

1.   On the **Standard** toolbar, click 🖼 **Open**.

2.   Locate the **kit_complete.dpp** file and click **Open**.

The drawing will open showing a line drawing created in the tutorial *Penning a Sketch* on p. 65.

Applying hand-drawn pressure

The lines on our drawing are all identical in thickness (2.4pt weight). This may work for a variety of illustrations, but we want to simulate the variation of thickness you'd achieve with a physical pen and paper.

As we progress through this tutorial we'll work with one simple rule:

•   Where a line joins another line at a dead-end, the ending line is thicker at the join.

We'll be simulating hand-drawn pressure using the preset profiles available on the Pressure tab. So let's get started...

To add a preset pressure profile:

1.   (Optional) On the **HintLine** toolbar, click ⊕ **Zoom In** or drag the Zoom slider to the right to zoom into the head of the drawing.

2.   On the **Drawing** toolbar, from the Pointer Tool flyout, click the ⬉ **Pointer Tool**.

3. Click once to select the left-hand section of the hat.

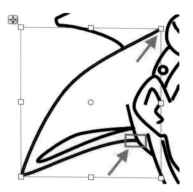

As you can see the line joins another line at one end but not the other. Therefore we'll apply a pressure profile which reflects this.

4. On the **Pressure** tab, from the preset profiles drop-down list, select the descending linear gradient profile (see below).

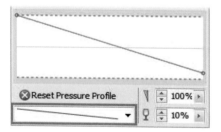

The line now appears thicker where it dead-ends and tapers off at the other end.

That looks much better, however the dead-end line thickness is still identical to the line it joins. This is because the top of the pressure profile graph indicates the weight of the line set on the Line tab. We'll change this now...

To change line weight:

- With the line still selected, on the **Line** tab, increase the weight to around **4.5pt**.

That's the first line done!

Adjusting pressure

There will be a few occasions when the preset profile doesn't quite
fit the varying thickness of the line you are seeking. We applied a
variety of profiles and line weights to our character's hat but the
right-hand extension didn't look quite right.

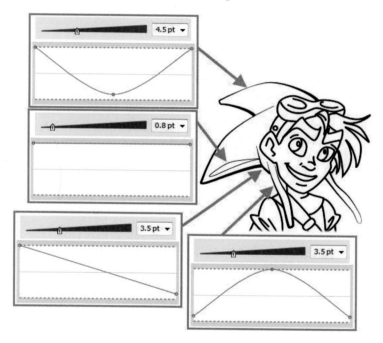

We want the thickness at the base of the extension to mirror that
of the left-hand extension, but the tops need to be thicker as they
join with the character's face.

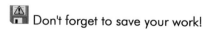 Don't forget to save your work!

To adjust a preset pressure profile:

1. With the **Pointer Tool**, click to select the right-hand hat extension.

2. On the **Line** tab, increase the weight to around **5pt** and, on the **Pressure** tab, from the preset profiles drop-down list, select the reverse bell-shaped (Gaussian) curve (shown below).

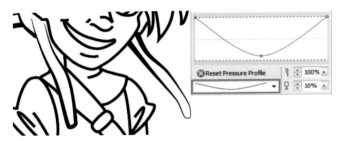

The line is too thin at the base—we can change this by adjusting the profile's graph.

3. On the **Pressure** tab:

    *   Click and drag the graph's middle point up towards the central dividing line.

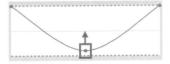

- Close to the left point, click on the graph to add another point, then drag it towards the central dividing line.

- Repeat the step above close to the right point.

With the pressure profile adjusted, the line looks much better.

Don't forget to save your work!

Continue applying pressure

You can now apply preset pressure profiles to the remainder of
the illustration's lines and adjust them as necessary.

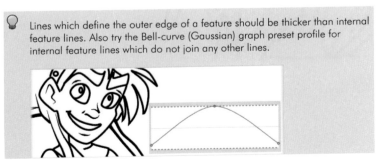

Lines which define the outer edge of a feature should be thicker than internal
feature lines. Also try the Bell-curve (Gaussian) graph preset profile for
internal feature lines which do not join any other lines.

That's it! Your simulated hand-drawn illustration is complete.

Brushes

 25-35 min

The Brushes tab in DrawPlus includes a wide selection of pressure-sensitive, artistic brushes, which you can use to create some impressive effects.

We'll introduce you to this exciting collection of drawing tools and show you how to use the brushes in your drawings.

By the end of this tutorial you will be able to:

- Convert lines to brush strokes and draw with brush strokes.

- Edit brush lines.

- Change brush stroke attributes.

You can either create your own drawing or follow our tutorial exactly by working from the resource file below.

 Go to **http://go.serif.com/resources/DPX6** to download the following resource file(s):

 bunny.dpp

Let's begin...

1. On the **Standard** toolbar, click 📋 **Open**.

2. Locate **bunny.dpp** and click **Open**.

At the moment, the bunny looks like a cartoon drawn with QuickShapes as it has smooth vector outlines.

There are two ways that we can give it a hand-drawn look:

*   Convert the existing lines to brush strokes using the **Line** tab.

*   Use the original lines as a guide (on Layer 1), and trace over them with the 🖌 Brush Tool (on another layer).

🛑 **Save now!** Click **File** > **Save As** and choose a new name for your file.

To convert lines to brush strokes:

1. With the ➤ **Pointer Tool**, click and drag to create a selection around the bunny. On release, the objects are selected.

2. On the **Line** tab:

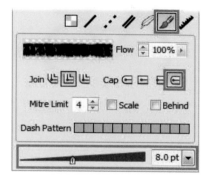

- Click the 🖌 **Brush Stroke** button. The default brush stroke is applied.

- Change the **Cap** style to ⊏ **Projecting Line Cap**.

- Drag the slider to increase the line width to **8** pt. (Or type 8 into the Width input box.)

3. On the **Brushes** tab, in the drop-down brush category list, click **Draw**.

4. Finally, click the **Graphic Soft Outline 03** brush. Immediately, the illustration takes on a hand-drawn effect!

 The illustration above shows the brush lines at a zoom level of 40% and 200%, respectively.

 Don't forget to save your work!

The Brush tool

The 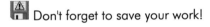 Brush Tool allows you to draw or paint with natural looking lines. DrawPlus includes ✐ 'stroke' and ☁ 'spray' brushes, stored on the Brushes tab. Brushes are divided into categories depending on their appearance. We'll be focussing on the ones in the Draw category.

The ✐ **Brush Tool** and the available brushes (and also the ✐ **Pencil Tool**) are pressure sensitive and will look very natural when used with either a pen and graphics tablet, or by using a combination of the mouse and **Pressure** tab. Search *Pressure sensitivity* in DrawPlus Help for more information or see *Simulating Hand-Drawn Pressure* on p. 81.

A pen and tablet works in a similar way to pencil and paper! With the pen, press and drag on the tablet to draw a line. Lift the pen to stop drawing. If you want a heavy, thick line, press hard on the tablet. For a thin, light line, use the pen lightly on the tablet. To select a line (or object, button etc.), hover the cursor over the line and then tap the pen on the tablet (this is the same as clicking with the left mouse button). You can also fine-tune any line using the **Pressure** tab. For the greatest control, don't forget to set up your tablet using the **Pressure Studio**. Search *Using pen tablets* in DrawPlus Help for more information

We'll trace our QuickShape drawing onto a new layer to achieve the results similar to that displayed in the example below.

To make the bunny easier to trace, we first selected all the objects on Layer 1 and, on the **Colour** tab, we reduced the line **Opacity** to **30%**.

To draw with the Brush Tool:

1. On the **Standard** toolbar, click 📋 **Open** and locate the original **bunny.dpp** file and click **Open**.

2. On **Layers** tab, click ⊹ **Add Layer**. A new layer is added above Layer 1.

3. On the **Hintline** toolbar, use the Zoom buttons (or slider) to zoom into your drawing so that the bunny fills most of the workspace.

4. On the **Drawing** toolbar, click the 🖌 **Brush Tool** and then on the **Brushes** tab, in the drop-down brush category list, click **Draw**.

5. Click the **Graphic Soft Outline 03** brush. This is a 🖌 'stroke' bush, which is particularly good for drawing outlines.

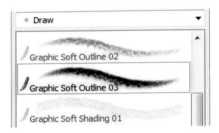

6. On the context toolbar, set the **Width** to 8 pt, and the **Smoothness** to 40%.

7. On the **Line** tab:

- Set the **Cap** to ⊆ **Projecting Line Cap**.

- Set the **Join** to ⊫ **Rounded Join**.

8. Use your pen and tablet (or mouse) to trace the first line by
    dragging on the page with the  brush cursor.

9. Continue to trace around the outline of the bunny.

Don't forget to save your work!

Editing brush lines and attributes

If you make a mistake on any of you lines (as we have done), you can quickly edit the path of the line with the ▷ **Node Tool**. Let's look at this briefly now.

To edit a brush line:

1. With the ✐ brush cursor, click to select the brush stroke that you want to edit.

2. To temporarily switch to the ▷ **Node Tool**, click and hold the **Ctrl** key.

3. Click and drag on the line and the control handles until the line is correctly positioned.

Once you've completed your outline, you can also use the brushes to shade, paint or 'colour in' your drawing.

 For more details on creating and modifying lines, see *Penning a Sketch* on p. 65.

Don't forget to save your work!

Applying colour using a brush

The  'spray' brushes are great for quickly filling in large blocks of colour, while the 'stroke' brushes tend to work best for cross-hatching and more traditional shading techniques.

To 'colour-in' with a brush:

1. On **Layers** tab, click ⊕ **Add Layer**. A new layer is added above Layer 2. (We also hid Layer 1 by clicking ⬤.)

2. On the **Hintline** toolbar, use the Zoom buttons (or slider) to zoom into your drawing so that the bunny fills most of the workspace.

3. On the **Drawing** toolbar, click the 🖌 **Brush Tool**.

4. On the **Brushes** tab, in the drop-down brush category list, click **Draw**.

5.   Click the **Chalk - Soft** brush. This is a 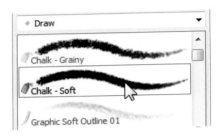 'spray' bush, which is particularly good for shading.

Draw

Chalk - Grainy

Chalk - Soft

Graphic Soft Outline 01

6.   On the context toolbar, set the **Width** to **6** pt and the **Smoothness** to around **20%**.

7.   On the **Line** tab, set the **Cap** to ⊑ **Projecting Line Cap** and the **Join** to ⤶ **Rounded Join**.

8.   Click and drag on the page, in the same way as you would shade in a drawing on paper, to shade in the pupil of the eye.

9. We can add some colour by simply changing the line colour on the **Colour** or **Swatch** tab. Here, we set the line to pink and coloured-in the nose.

Repeat the process, changing the brush type, colour and brush width until you have completely coloured-in your drawing.

10. Finally, on the **Layers** tab, click **Move Layer Down** to move Layer 3 below Layer 2. Your lines will now be on top of the coloured areas!

Don't forget to save your work!

There's so much more you can do!

Below are some examples of what else you can do...

Add background and foreground elements

We applied a dark brown colour to our bunny's outline and created a background using a soft smudge brush for the sky, and a realistic grass brush from the brushes Photo category. See the following tutorial, *Spray Painting*, for more inspiration.

Create sketched text

You don't have to stick with drawings, you can also use brushes to add stylish effects to text!

Spray Painting

 15-20 min

As we've seen in *Brushes* on p. 89, the Brushes tab includes a wide selection of artistic brushes. Spray brushes in particular are great for filling in and shading large areas, just as an airbrush would be in the non-digital world. Many of the DrawPlus spray brushes create photo-realistic textures on the page.

By the end of this tutorial you will be able to:

*   Use layers to control the depth of the painting.

*   Use a variety of spray brushes.

*   Export a completed image to a new file.

 Go to **http://go.serif.com/resources/DPX6** to download the following resource file(s):

chapel.dpp

Let's begin...

1. On the **Standard** toolbar, click ☐ **Open**.

2. Locate the **chapel.dpp** file and click **Open**.

The drawing opens in your workspace.

We'll use a selection of spray brushes to build up a background and foreground for our scene.

📌 We drew the chapel using the **Pen Tool** by tracing over a photograph.

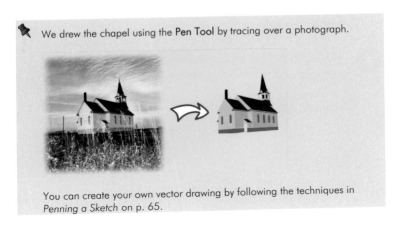

You can create your own vector drawing by following the techniques in *Penning a Sketch* on p. 65.

Using layers to build up a drawing

To create our finished image, we're going to add various brush strokes to the Background and Foreground layers within the drawing. The vector drawing of the chapel is located on a middle layer (named Chapel), locked to prevent unintentional changes.

 Search *Working with layers* in DrawPlus Help for more information on adding, deleting, and using layers.

We have already added a blue Quick Rectangle (representing the sky) to the Background layer to save you time. See *Basic QuickShapes* on p. 13 for more information.

Using several layers within a design means we can work on specific areas of the painting without the fear of accidentally modifying other areas.

Using textured spray brushes

On the **Brushes** tab, the spray brushes are denoted with the
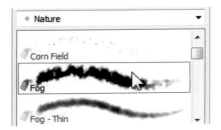 icon. Spray brushes may be based on images (p. 108) or
textures. Both can be recoloured.

We'll start by using a brush to add a few clouds to the sky line.

To add the clouds:

1. On the **Layers** tab, click on the **Background** layer to make it
   the active layer.

2. On the **Drawing** toolbar, click the Brush Tool.

3. On the **Brushes** tab, in the drop-down brush category list, click
   Nature and then, click the **Fog** brush.

4. On the **Swatch** tab, click the **Line** button and then click the
   white swatch.

5. At the top of the workspace, on the context toolbar, set the
   brush **Width** to **250** pt and the **Opacity** to **50%**.

6. Click and drag a zigzag line across the top of page to paint a layer of cloud in the sky. Don't worry if the paint extends off the page.

The cloud appears behind the chapel as it's on the layer below the **Chapel** layer.

7. On the context toolbar, increase the **Opacity** to **100%** and click and drag another line across the page.

An illusion of depth is created due to the varying opacity of each cloud.

Now, let's add another layer of clouds to define the horizon.

Save now! Click **File > Save As** and choose a new name for your file.

To define the horizon:

1. On the **Brushes** tab, in the drop-down brush category list, click **Effects** and then, click the **Clouds** brush.

2. On the context toolbar, set the **Width** to **99** pt.

3. Click and drag across the page to define the horizon with a line of clouds.

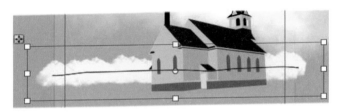

4. (Optional) Add extra depth to the horizon by adding another painted line over the clouds, using **Fog - thin** (**Nature** category), set to **190** pt and a shade of grey.

Your layers of clouds are now finished!

Currently the chapel looks to be floating in the sky! Let's bring it down to earth by adding some foliage behind the building.

To add foliage:

1. On the **Brushes** tab, in the **Nature** category, click the **Trees** brush.

   The brush is great for quickly creating foliage.

2. On the context toolbar, set the brush **Width** to **20** pt and the **Opacity** to **100%**.

3. Click and drag a free-flowing line at the horizon to create foliage on both sides of the chapel.

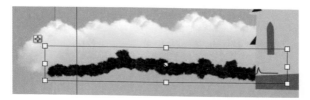

The chapel looks much more grounded now! Before we move onto the foreground, it's worth experimenting with other brushes in the Brushes tab to create other landscape features.

We used the **Wash - Round** brush from the **Paint** category (set to a **Width** of **25** pt and coloured brown) to create the wooden fence to finish the background.

Don't forget to save your work!

Using image-based spray brushes

We'll fill in the foreground with brush which resembles springy, green moss and then add a feature using an image-based grass brush to complete the painting.

To add moss:

1. On the **Layers** tab, click on the **Foreground** layer.

2. On the **Brushes** tab, in the **Nature** category, click the **Moss** brush.

3. On the context toolbar, set the brush **Width** to **40** pt and the **Opacity** to **100%**.

4. Click and drag back and forth across the lower part of the painting to fill the entire area with 'moss'.

Be careful not to cover too much of the lower layers when painting.

To add image-based brush lines:

1. On the **Brushes** tab, in the **Photo** category, click the **Grass** brush.

2. On the context toolbar, set the **Width** to **200** pt and the **Opacity** to **100%**.

3. On the **Swatch** tab, click the **Line** button and then select a yellow swatch (so the grass resembles wheat).

4. Click and drag back and forth across the base of the painting to add a thick line of wheat.

5. (Optional) On the context toolbar, increase the **Width** to **255** pt and add a few extra strands of wheat on top of the previous brush stroke.

That's it! Your spray brush painting is complete!

Don't forget to save your work!

Exporting your finished image

As you can see, we've extended past the boundaries of the page. This doesn't matter as DrawPlus will tidy things up when we export the image.

To export an image to a new file:

1. On the **File** menu, click **Export > Export as Picture**.

2. In the **Picture Export** dialog:

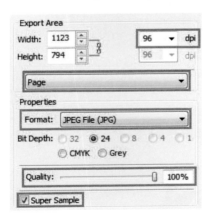

- The **Export Area** shows the dimensions of your current image in pixels at the displayed 96dpi (dots per inch). To change the printed resolution, increase or decrease the dpi.

- Ensure that the **Page** option is selected from the drop-down list.

- Choose the file type from the **Format** drop-down list and set the output quality if applicable (as in our example).

- Select **Super Sample** (if available) to improve the look of lines.

- Click **Export**.

3. To complete the export, browse to the folder in which you want to create the file, give it a file name and click **Save**.

 The options available in the **Picture Export** dialog are dependent on the export format that has been selected. Search *Exporting objects and drawings* in DrawPlus Help for more details.

You should now have an image that resembles ours.

We hope you've enjoyed working with the spray brushes. Remember, the best way to find out what each brush does is to experiment freely. Have fun!

There's so much more you can do!

Below are some examples of what else you can do...

Combine paint and photos

You can apply some fantastic effects to photos using the brushes in DrawPlus! The example above uses **Grunge 01** brush from the **Grunge** category.

Add an edge effect

Simply select your photo and then on the **Brushes** tab, click to select a brush from the **Edges** category.

Creating Navigation Buttons

15-20 min

When you hover over a navigation button on a website, you'll often see the button's appearance change. This is controlled by a clever bit of code and different graphics known as **rollover states**. DrawPlus creates all of the code for you, you just need to create the design!

By the end of this tutorial you will be able to:

*   Create slice objects and set button properties and states.

*   Preview your finished web button in a web browser.

*   Apply actions to buttons.

*   Export your web button and its rollover states.

We have created the starting button for you to download.

 Go to **http://go.serif.com/resources/DPX6** to download the following resource file(s):

 button.dpp

Let's begin...

1. On the **Standard** toolbar, click **Open**.

2. Locate **button.dpp** and click **Open**.

> For this project, we have used a custom page setup with the ruler units set to pixels. Setting a specific page size is a good habit to get into when you are designing for a particular output such as for web buttons, icons and even logos. For more on changing ruler units and setting page size, search *Setting measurement units and drawing scale* in DrawPlus Help.

Save now! Click **File** > **Save As** and choose a new name for your file.

Creating a web object

A rollover button is simply an image that has different states which are triggered by a mouse-over action or with a mouse click. Luckily, it's really easy to create these states in DrawPlus.

As you can see, we have created a "recycle" button graphic using a collection of different objects.

These objects will become the starting image for our rollover button, known as the Normal rollover state, i.e., the appearance of the button when there is no mouse action taking place.

The next step is to change the graphic into a web object. To do this, we need to create a sliced object.

To create and adjust a sliced object:

1. On the **Insert** menu, click **Web Object>Image Slice**.

2. With the ✛🖊 cursor, click and drag over the button to set the approximate size of the slice object.

On release, slice lines are displayed on the page defining the button as a separate web object.

On the **Layers** tab, you will notice that a new **Web Layer** has been created.

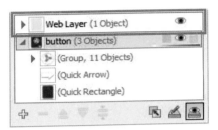

3. On the **Layers** tab, select the **Web Layer** and then, on the page, select the blue slice object with the ↖ **Pointer Tool**.

4. Drag the handles of the slice object so that they line up with the edges of the image.

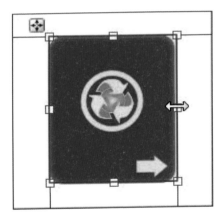

You can also insert a slice object from the right-click menu. Select your button first, and then on the right-click menu click **Insert Slice Object**. The slice area is immediately created at the correct size for the object. (Certain filter effects may cause the slice object to appear larger than the actual object dimensions due to the effect "bleed". In this case, you will need to adjust the slice manually.)

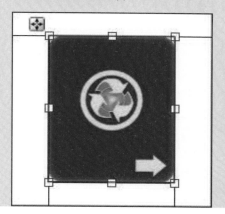

 Don't forget to save your work!

Creating button 'states'

Now that our button is defined as a web object, we need to define its rollover states. This will allow us to apply different graphics to each state.

To define rollover states:

1. On the **Layers** tab, ensure that the **Web Layer** is selected and on the page, double-click the shaded region of the slice object. The **Image Slice Object Properties** dialog opens.

2. In the **Rollover Details** section, click to select the **Over** and **Down** check boxes and click **OK**.

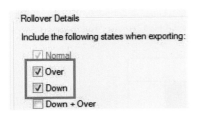

3. On the **Layers** tab, you'll now see four layers in the drawing:

- **Web Layer**—containing the image slice object.

- **Down (Down)**

- **Over (Over)**

- **button (Normal)**—containing the button.

On the **Layers** tab, if you select the **Down** or **Over** layer, you'll see that they are empty. As we already have a graphic on our **Normal** layer, we can use this to create a **variant state** (a different graphic) on the **Over** and **Down** layers.

To create rollover states:

1. On the **Layers** tab, click 👁 **Visible** to hide the **Web Layer**.

2. Click to select the **button (Normal)** layer.

3. With the 🖈 **Pointer Tool**, drag a selection around the entire button, and press **Ctrl + C** to copy.

4. On the **Layers** tab, select the **Over** layer. Press **Ctrl + V** to paste the copied objects. An exact copy of the objects is pasted in place.

5. Next, click to select the **Down** layer. Press **Ctrl + V** to paste the copied objects to this layer also.

   You should now have an exact copy of the button on each of the three 'state' layers (which you can see by expanding each layer as we have done).

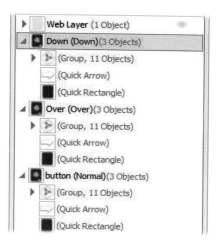

At the moment, each state is an exact copy. So that something happens when we use our button, let's make a change to the **Over** state.

6. On the **Layers** tab, select the **Over (Over)** layer and then, click the central grouped object.

7. Press the **Ctrl** key while dragging on a corner handle to increase the size of the object while keeping the centre in the same place.

8. Click to select the Quick Arrow at the bottom of the button, and on the **Colour** tab, adjust the colour wheel to apply an orange fill.

We'll leave the **Down** layer as it is so that the button returns to the same state when it is clicked.

 Don't forget to save your work!

Previewing a rollover button

Now that our three states are complete, we can preview the button in a web browser.

To preview a button:

1. On the **File** menu, click **Preview in Browser**.

2. In the **Preview in Browser** dialog, select **Image Slices** option and click **OK**.

    This launches your default browser and displays the button.

3. Roll your mouse over the button to see the variant 'Over' graphic you defined.

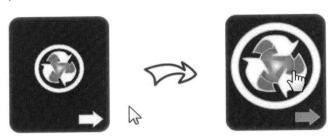

4. Close the browser window when you have finished previewing your button.

Applying actions (events) to a button

If you click the button in the browser, you may either receive an error message or notice no action takes place. This is because there is no URL link specified for the button. We'll show you how to set a link and specify some rollover text now.

To apply button actions:

1. On the **Layers** tab, select the **Web Layer** and click ✳ **Visible** to make it visible.

2. Right-click the shaded region of the slice object and click **Properties**.

   The **Image Slice Object Properties** dialog opens.

3. In the **URL Details** section:

    •   Type a **URL** for your button to point to (for example www.recycle.com).

    •   Type some descriptive text. This will appear when you point to the button. (For example 'Learn more about recycling'.)

    •   Click **OK**.

4. Preview you button again to see the changes in action.

Don't forget to save your work!

Exporting your button

To complete the process of creating a web button, we need to export it. Let's do this now.

To export the complete rollover button:

1. On the **Web** layer, select the slice object and on the **File** menu, click **Export** > **Export as Picture**.

2. In the **Picture Export** dialog:

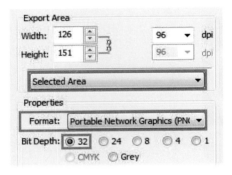

*   In the **Export Area** section, select **Selected Area** from the drop-down list.

*   In the **Properties** section, in the **Format** drop-down list, select an appropriate file type (typically GIF, JPEG, or PNG) and choose your settings. (We selected **32** bit **PNG**).

- In the **Web Options** section, ensure the **Image Slices** check box is selected.

- Click **Export**.

3. In the **Export** dialog, select a location for your exported files (we recommend creating a folder first). Type a name for your button (e.g., navbtn) and click **Save**.

Congratulations, you've exported your web button along with its rollover states!

DrawPlus creates a file for each image state, and a single file containing the HTML code, from which you can copy and paste <head> and <body> sections into the corresponding sections of your web page.

If you now open your folder, the contents should resemble ours. (The appearance of the files depends on your settings and your current default browser—in our example, we have file extensions visible and the default browser is IE.)

 navbtn.html
HTML Document
3.92 KB

 navbtn.png
PNG Image
9.71 KB

 navbtn_d.png
PNG Image
9.71 KB

 navbtn_h.png
PNG Image
16.8 KB

Colour & Opacity

Colour and Opacity are fundamental in adding depth and excitement to illustrations and design. DrawPlus provides a variety of ways to add colour and adjust opacity within your designs and we'll explore some of these ways in this section.

Solid Fills

5-10 min

In this tutorial we are going to add a splash of solid colour to our drawings to make them stand out!

By the end of this tutorial you will be able to:

- Navigate between pages of a multi-page drawing.

- Copy multiple objects.

- Change the colour of lines and fills using the Swatch and Colour tabs.

- Use the Format Painter to copy fill and line properties.

If you've completed *Basic QuickShapes* (p. 13) or *Modifying Shapes* (p. 31), you can use your saved projects as a starting point for this tutorial. Otherwise, you can use the resource file provided.

 Go to **http://go.serif.com/resources/DPX6** to download the following resource file(s):

🔽 quickshapes.dpp

Let's begin...

1. On the **Standard** toolbar, click ☐ **Open**.

2. Locate **quickshapes.dpp** and click **Open**.

3. On the **Hintline** toolbar, click ▸ **Next Page** to reach **Page** 2.

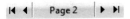

    The page displays a flower at its centre.

We will look at applying solid colour fills to our shapes. For this, we'll introduce the Swatch and Colour tabs.

Colour using the Swatch tab

First, we are going to add colour to a copy of our flower.

To copy objects:

1. On the **Drawing** toolbar, from the Pointer Tool flyout, click the ▸ Pointer Tool.

2. Click and drag on the page to create a selection around the flower.

On release, the objects are selected.

3. Hold the **Ctrl** key and drag the selected objects.

Release the mouse button before the **Ctrl** key to complete the copy—on release, the new objects are selected.

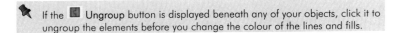

If the Ungroup button is displayed beneath any of your objects, click it to ungroup the elements before you change the colour of the lines and fills.

To apply a solid fill and line colour:

1. With the ↖ **Pointer Tool**, click to select the petals.

2. On the **Swatch** tab, the  **Document Palette** is displayed by default.

- Click the **Line** button and then, click a dark blue swatch.

- Click the **Fill** button and then, click a lighter blue swatch.

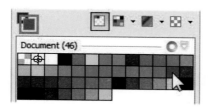

The flower petals are filled with the new colours.

3. Click to select the flower centre. Repeat step 2 to apply an orange outline and a yellow fill.

4. Click to select the flower stem. On the **Swatch** tab, click the arrow on the **Palettes** button and select **Standard RGB** from the drop-down list. Click the **Line** button and then, click a dark green swatch.

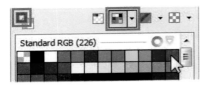

If you have problems when selecting objects which are obscured, press the **Alt** key while clicking.

5. Finally, select the leaves. On the **Swatch** tab, apply a dark green line, and a lighter green fill. (If you can't find a colour that you like, try selecting a different palette.)

Your flower is complete!

Any colours that are used in your drawing are added to the **Document Palette** so that they are easy to find and reuse!

 Save now! Click **File** > **Save As** and choose a new name for your file.

Copying colour formatting

Next, we're going to look at copying formatting from one object to another. We're going to use another flower for this.

To copy line and colour formatting:

1.   Create another copy of the original flower (see p. 130).

2. With the ⬉ **Pointer Tool**, click to select the coloured leaves of your coloured flower, and then on the **Standard** toolbar, click ⬛ **Format Painter**.

3. Click on the black and white leaves of the copied flower.

They update immediately.

4. Repeat this technique to colour the stem and centre of the flower.

 The ⊤ **Format Painter** applies the colour and line properties (including weight, type, opacity, etc.) to an object. It doesn't affect the size of shape. Search *Copying an object's formatting* in DrawPlus Help for more information about the Format Painter.

 Don't forget to save your work!

Colour using the Colour tab

You can apply colour to any object using the Colour tab. This is perfect for 'mixing' your own colours, rather than relying on the presets available from the Swatch tab.

To apply a solid fill and line colour:

1. With the ↖ **Pointer Tool**, click to select the black and white petals of the copied flower.

2. On the **Colour** tab:

   • From the mode drop-down list, select **HSL Colour Wheel**.

   • Click the **Line** button and then click and drag the black circle in the outer wheel to change the Hue. Click in the triangle to select a colour saturation and lightness.

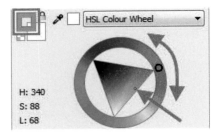

- Click the **Fill** button and then, repeat the process above to select a lighter fill colour.

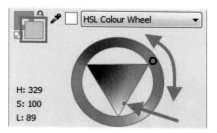

Your second flower is complete!

 When choosing line colours for cartoons, instead of using black, try a darker version of your fill colour. We think you'll be pleased with the results!

That's it! Now you know how to add solid colour fills to objects on the page. You can now print your flowers, export them, or copy them to the Gallery tab to use in other DrawPlus projects. Search *Printing basics*, *Exporting objects and drawings*, and *Using the Gallery* in DrawPlus Help for more details.

 Don't forget to save your work!

There's so much more you can do!

Below are some examples of what else you can do...

Colour some animals

We used a combination of these three fill techniques to colour the cartoon animals created in *Modifying Shapes* on p. 31. Why not give it a try yourself?

Colour a vector line drawing

You can use solid fills to colour line illustrations! See *Penning a Sketch* on p. 65 for more information on creating vector line drawings.

Gradient Fills

 25-30 min

Gradient fills can quickly add a lot more depth to your drawings by creating subtle shading. Although this tutorial concentrates on fills, gradient can be applied to lines in exactly the same way!

By the end of this tutorial you will be able to:

- Replicate an object.

- Apply gradient fills from the Swatch tab and with the Fill Tool.

- Edit gradient fill colours and use the Fill Tool to edit paths.

- Save a gradient fill for later use.

If you've completed *Solid Fills* on p. 129, you can use your saved project as a starting point for this tutorial. Otherwise, you can use the resource file provided.

 Go to **http://go.serif.com/resources/DPX6** to download the following resource file(s):

🔽 **quickshapes.dpp**

Let's begin...

1. On the **Standard** toolbar, click 📤 **Open**.

2. Locate **quickshapes.dpp** and click **Open**.

3. On the **Hintline** toolbar, continue clicking ▶ **Next Page** to reach **Page** 3.

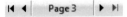

The page displays a coloured flower at its centre.

We will look at applying gradient colour fills to our shapes. For this, we'll introduce the Swatch tab and Fill Tool.

Gradient fills

The following example shows a few different gradient fills that would suit our QuickShape flowers—Solid, Linear, Radial, Three Colour, and Four Colour (from left to right).

There are several ways to apply gradient fills, let's look at those now.

We'll apply each new gradient to a copy of the blue flower we created in *Solid Fills* on p. 129. The quickest way to create multiple copies is by using the Replicate option.

To replicate an object:

1. Click and drag on the page to create a selection around the flower.

On release, the objects are selected.

2. From the **Tools** menu, select **Replicate**.

3. In the **Replicate** dialog, set the **Columns** to 2 and **Rows** to 2 and click **OK**.

Three copies of the flower appear on the page.

Now let's look at gradient fills from the Swatch tab's perspective...

Save now! Click **File > Save As** and choose a new name for your file.

To apply a gradient fill (Swatch tab):

1. With the **Pointer Tool**, select the petals on one of the blue flowers.

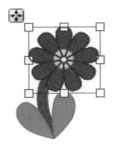

2. On the **Swatch** tab, click arrow on the ▨ ▾ **Gradient** button and select **Conical** from the drop-down list.

3. Click the ▤ **Fill** button and then, click a blue gradient swatch to apply the gradient.

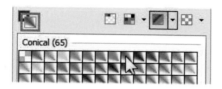

The gradient fill is applied to the petals of the flower.

Now we'll apply a gradient fill using the Fill Tool...

To apply a linear gradient fill (Fill Tool):

1. With the ↖ **Pointer Tool**, select the petals on one of the blue flowers.

2. On the **Drawing** toolbar, click the ◈ **Fill Tool**.

3. On the context toolbar, ensure that ▬ **Apply to Fill** is selected.

4. Drag from one side of the petals to the other to apply a linear gradient.

By default, your current fill colour will be used as the start colour, and the end colour will be white.

You can also apply gradient fills to lines!

On the context toolbar, ensure ☐ **Apply to Line** is selected, then use the 🔷 **Fill Tool** in exactly the same way as if you were applying the gradient to the object's fill.

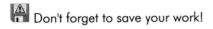 Don't forget to save your work!

Editing gradient fills with the Fill Tool

You can edit a gradient fill at any time. Clicking a new gradient swatch on the Swatch tab will replace the current fill. To edit the current fill, you need to use the Fill Tool.

To change a fill type:

1. With the ▸ **Pointer Tool**, select the petals on one of the blue flowers.

2. On the **Drawing** toolbar, click the ◈ **Fill Tool**.

3. On the context toolbar, from the Fill Style drop-down list, select **Radial**.

Now to update the colours...

To change key colours (context toolbar method):

1. With the petals and  **Fill Tool** still selected, on the context toolbar, select a new colour from the **Start Colour** drop-down list (we chose orange).

2. Select a new colour from the **End Colour** drop-down list (we chose a pale blue).

To change key colours (path handles and tab method):

* With the petals and **Fill Tool** still selected, select a path handle with the ⊿₊ cursor, and then on the **Swatch** (or **Colour**) tab, click a new colour (we chose red).

> Depending on the type of fill applied (linear, radial, ellipse, etc.), a fill path is displayed as one or more lines, with handles marking where the spectrum between each key colour begins and ends.

Now we'll take you through adding and deleting colours to your gradient and changing the gradient spread.

 Don't forget to save your work!

To add a key colour:

- With the petals and 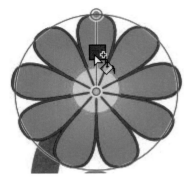 Fill Tool still selected, drag a colour swatch from the **Swatch** tab onto a portion of the fill path where there is no handle. The cursor changes to include a plus (+) sign.

- Release the mouse button to add a new handle to the fill path using the chosen colour.

To delete a key colour:

- Select a colour handle and press the **Delete** key.

To change the colour spread:

- Click and drag the fill path handles.
  - or -

- Drag the start and end path handles.
  - or -

- Click on a new location for the start handle and drag out a new fill path.

That's it! Now you know how to add and adjust gradient colour fills. You can now print your flowers, export them, or copy them to the Gallery tab to use in other DrawPlus projects. Search *Printing basics*, *Exporting objects and drawings*, and *Using the Gallery* in DrawPlus Help for more details.

 Don't forget to save your work!

Saving a gradient fill

Once you've created your customized gradient fill, you can save it
for use in later projects.

To save a gradient fill:

1. On the **Swatch** tab, select the 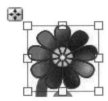 **Document Palette**.

2. With the **Pointer Tool**, select the object containing the fill you
    want to save.

3. On the **Swatch** tab, click the ▽ **Palette Menu**, and select **Add
    Fill from Selection**.

4. In the **Add Fill To Studio** dialog, type a name for your fill and
    click **OK**.

    Your fill is added to the **Document Palette**.

Mesh Fills

 5-10 min

The details of working with mesh fills is covered extensively in *Working with mesh fills* in DrawPlus Help. However, in this tutorial we'll help you apply and update a simple mesh fill to give natural colouring to an object.

By the end of this tutorial you will be able to:

• Use a mesh fill to add natural colour blends.

• Use a mesh fill to add depth.

We recommend using the resource file provided so we can concentrate on the main learning point of this tutorial.

 Go to **http://go.serif.com/resources/DPX6** to download the following resource file(s):

🔾 **mesh.dpp**

Let's begin...

1. On the **Standard** toolbar, click **Open**.

2. Locate **mesh.dpp** and click **Open**.

    The page displays a coloured pear at its centre.

We have already applied solid fills to both the fruit and the stalk. See *Solid Fills* on p. 129 for details.

> The pear was created in *Modifying Shapes* on p. 31 and the stalk was created from combining a Quick Polygon with a Quick Star (see *Building a Dragon with Shapes* on p. 41 for details).

Applying a mesh fill

It is very rare to find anything in nature which is a single colour. Most natural objects contain several tones of colour and to replicate this digitally we can use a mesh fill.

We also recommend zooming into your objects before editing a mesh fill as it will provide you with maximum control.

To add a second colour to a mesh fill:

1. On the **Drawing** toolbar, from the Pointer Tool flyout, click the **Pointer Tool** and then click to select the pear.

2. (Optional) On the **Hintline** toolbar, click ⊕ **Zoom In** (or use the Zoom slider) until the shape fills most of the screen.

3. On the **Drawing** toolbar, from the Fill Tool flyout, click the
    Mesh Fill Tool.

    A mesh displays around the pear shape.

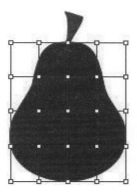

4. With the **Shift** key pressed down, select the nodes indicated below.

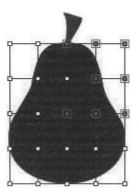

5. On the **Swatch** tab, from the ▾ **Palettes** drop-down list, select **Mid Tones**.

6. Click to select a red swatch (we chose C=48, M=82, Y=47, K=31).

   The colour under the selected nodes updates.

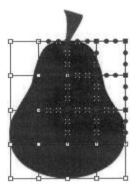

The red colour gradually blends with the previously applied green colour to give a smooth transition between the tones, giving the object a naturally coloured appearance.

Next, we'll show you how you can use a mesh fill to add depth to an image.

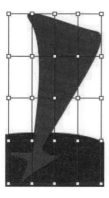 **Save now!** Click **File** > **Save As** and choose a new name for your file.

Adding depth

We'll use the same technique described previously to add a blended colour to the stalk to give the illusion the stalk is attached to the fruit.

To add depth using a mesh fill:

1. On the **Drawing** toolbar, from the Pointer Tool flyout, click the **Pointer Tool** and then click to select the stalk.

2. On the **Drawing** toolbar, from the Fill Tool flyout, click the **Mesh Fill Tool**.

    A mesh displays around the stalk shape.

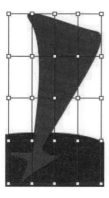

3. Click and drag a marquee to select the two bottom rows of nodes.

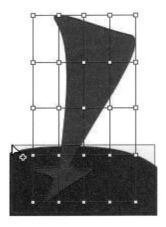

4. With the **Shift** key pressed down, click to deselect the node indicated below.

5. On the **Swatch** tab, select the 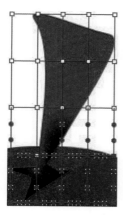 **Document Palette**, and then click to select a black swatch (we chose H=0, S=0, L=12).

The colour under the selected nodes updates.

6. Select the first four nodes in the top row and apply a yellow colour to complete the design (we chose C=16, M=10, Y=66, K=0 from the **Mid Tones** palette on the **Swatch** tab).

The black colour gives the impression the stalk is attached to the fruit and the yellow tone gives the stalk a natural look.

That's it! Now you know how to add colours to a mesh fill to give natural tones and depth to objects.

 Don't forget to save your work!

Creating Translucent Bubbles

 45-60 min

In this tutorial we'll explore some of the opacity and transparency settings available in DrawPlus. In the process we'll create a beautiful bubble which you can use in a variety of projects!

By the end of this tutorial you will be able to:

*   Create a background from a QuickShape.

*   Draw a perfect circle.

*   Apply and edit transparency.

*   Adjust a colour's opacity.

*   Add a feather edge to objects.

*   Retain opacity on exporting.

Let's begin...

- In the Startup Wizard, choose **Start New Drawing**, select a page size of your choice and click **OK**.

A blank page opens in your workspace.

Applying a background

As the bubbles we'll be creating are translucent, it's important for us to create a background to show them off. We can do this using a coloured Quick Rectangle.

To add a new layer:

1. On the **Layers** tab, click ⊹ **Add Layer**.

   A new layer, named Layer 2, is added to the tab.

2. Double-click Layer 2 and, in the **Layer Properties** dialog, type 'Background' in the **Name** text box and click **OK**.

   The Layers tab updates to display the layer's new name.

3. With the **Background** layer selected, on the **Layers** tab, click ▽ **Move Layer Down**.

   This will ensure anything added to the Background layer will display behind anything placed on Layer 1.

Now we'll add our background...

To add a background:

1. With the **Background** layer selected, on the **Drawing** toolbar, from the QuickShapes flyout, select ⬜ **Quick Rectangle**.

2. Position the cursor just above and to the left of the page and then click and drag so the rectangle fills the entire page.

3. On the **Colour** tab, click 🔒 **Link** to ensure the shape's line and fill colours are identical and then chose a colour using the HSL Colour Wheel.

The rectangle's colour updates, displaying a solid colour background.

Now we can focus on creating our bubbles!

🔲 **Save now!** Click **File > Save As** and choose a new name for your file.

Creating a bubble shape

When bubbles form they are spherical. We can replicate this by using a Quick Ellipse and constraining the shape to a circle.

To create a bubble shape:

1. With **Layer 1** selected, on the **Drawing** toolbar, from the QuickShapes flyout, select ⬤ **Quick Ellipse**.

2. Click and drag on the page while pressing down the **Shift** key (to constrain the shape) to draw a circle.

    The circle's line and fill colour will be identical to the background so the shape will be invisible!

3. On the **Colour** tab, click 🔒 **Link** so the shape's line and fill colours are independent, and set the **Fill** to white.

4. Click to select the **Line** and then click ⬚ **None** to remove any colour from the circle's line.

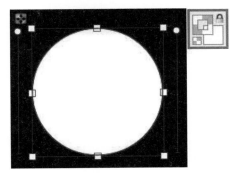

Now we'll add transparency to begin building up the bubble effect.

Applying transparency

There are a range of professionally designed transparency effects
you can apply with a single click from the Transparency tab.
However, we want more control over the transparency of our
bubble, so we'll use the Transparency Tool.

To apply transparency:

•   On the **Drawing** toolbar, select the ♀ **Transparency Tool**
    and, on the context toolbar, from the drop-down list, select
    Radial.

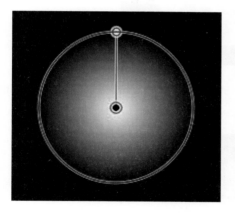

A radial transparency is added to the circle and the
transparency path is displayed.

Bubbles vary in opacity from transparent at the centre to almost
opaque at the edges—we need our transparency path to reflect
this.

To add handles to a transparency path:

1. On the context toolbar, set the **Opacity Start** to 0% and the **Opacity End** to 100%.

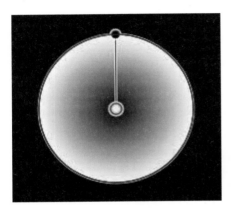

2. Place your cursor along the transparency path, just below the top handle—the cursor will change to 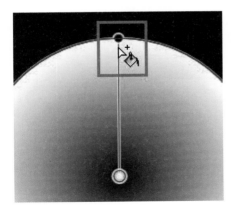.

3. Click once to add a handle to the transparency path—the new handle adopts the opacity value directly underneath it (as displayed on the context toolbar).

4. On the context toolbar, set the new handle's **Opacity** to 0%.

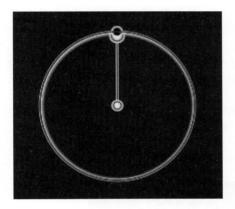

The bubble's structure has now been established.

Don't forget to save your work!

We'll add some depth by replicating the translucent circle and changing the transparency path...

To edit a transparency path:

1. On the **Drawing** toolbar, from the Pointer Tool flyout, click the
    ↖ **Pointer Tool** and click to select the circle.

2. Press **Ctrl+C** on your keyboard to copy the circle and then
    press **Ctrl+V** to paste a copy directly over the original.

3. With the copy still selected, on the **Drawing** toolbar, select the
    ♀ **Transparency Tool** to display its transparency path.

4. Click and drag to set the path as illustrated below.

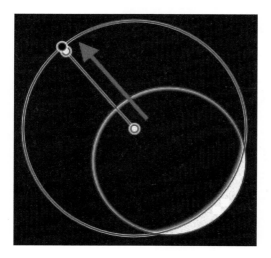

5. Click to select the middle handle and drag it down the path towards the centre to increase the transparency gradient.

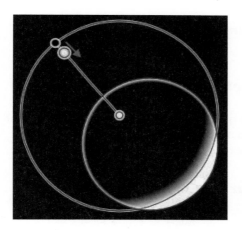

6. On the **Drawing** toolbar, click the ⬉ **Pointer Tool** and drag a selection around the circles.

7. Click **Group** ▣ to group the circles.

The bubble shape has now been created!

Next we'll add reflections to our bubble to enhance its 3D appearance!

 Don't forget to save your work!

Adding reflections

We'll explore the use of opacity (as a component of colour) and feathering on objects and add these to our bubble to give the impression of surface reflections.

To adjust a colour's opacity:

1. On the **Drawing** toolbar, select ⬭ **Quick Ellipse** and draw a small circle.

    It will automatically adopt the colour and transparency settings off the previously created circles.

2. On the **Transparency** tab, click the ▱ **None** swatch to remove any transparency from the shape.

3. On the **Colour** tab, ensure the Fill is selected and reduce the **Opacity** to **60%**.

The background colour will become partially visible through the circle's white fill.

4. Using the move button, click and drag the circle to position it inside the bubble.

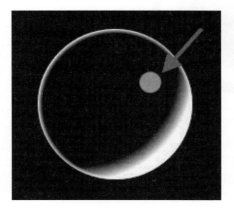

Now, we'll apply feathering to the circle's edge so it 'blends' better with the bubble.

🔺 Don't forget to save your work!

To add a feathered edge:

* With the circle still selected, on the **Styles** tab, drag the
  Feather Edge slider to the right to increase the blur on the
  circle's edge.

The inner reflective circle now blends well with the bubble.

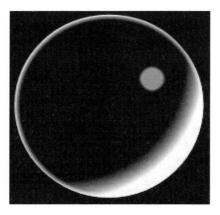

 Don't forget to save your work!

Completing the design

We completed our design by adding another smaller circle and a Quick Moon, and then applying opacity and feathered edges. We then grouped all the shapes together.

That's it! Your translucent bubble is complete.

 Don't forget to save your work!

You can now print the design or copy it to the Gallery tab to use in other DrawPlus projects. Search *Printing basics* and *Using the Gallery* in DrawPlus Help for more details.

Alternatively, you can export the bubble for external use while retaining its opacity.

To export with opacity:

1. With the grouped bubble selected, from the **File** menu, select Export > Export as Picture.

2. In the **Picture Export** dialog:

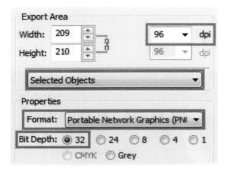

- From the dpi drop-down list select **96** for electronic use or **300** for printed use.

- In the **Export Area**'s drop-down list, select **Selected Objects**.

- From the **Format** drop-down list, select **Portable Network Graphics (PNG)**.

- Set the **Bit Depth** to **32** (this will retain opacity settings).

  The preview will update to display a white and grey chequered background to represent transparency.

- (Optional) Select **Super Sample** to improve the look of lines.

- Click **Export**.

3. To complete the export, browse to the folder in which you want to create the file, give it a file name and click **Save**.

You can now place the bubble in a website (as below) or other publication.

There's so much more you can do!

Below are some examples of what else you can do...

Transform your bubble and add some sparkle

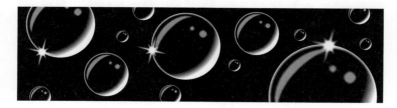

The **Transform** command from the **Tools** menu is perfect for quickly replicating and resizing your bubbles. Why not then use it as a background for other designs?

See *Transforming a Folding Fan* on p. 51 and or search *Applying a transform* in DrawPlus Help for more information.

Then why not give the illusion of light glancing from the bubble's surface by placing a Quick Star, with opacity and feathering applied, to the edge of some of the bubbles. We used four point stars with a **Minor Radius** of **52%** and an **Inner Radius** of **16%**.

Gradient fill the background

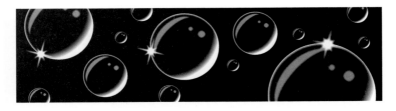

Rather than using a solid fill for the background, why not use a gradient fill? We used a preset from the **Automatic** (**Gradient**) palette from the **Swatch** tab.

Explore the Styles tab

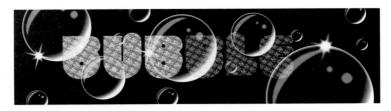

Delve in a little deeper into the **Styles** tab and you'll find a wealth of professionally designed styles you can instantly add to objects. Different Impressions, from the **Stamps** category, were applied to the text in the above example. Search *Using graphic styles* in DrawPlus Help for more information.

Typography

Typography is an essential part of design and illustration, particularly for business and advertising purposes. In this chapter we will guide you through the basic text objects at your disposal and then delve into customizing and modifying text to create some beautiful typographical designs.

Artistic, Shape and Frame Text

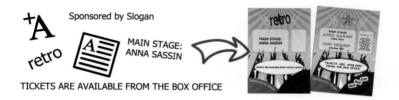 25-35 min

DrawPlus offers three types of text to use in your projects, frame text, shape text and artistic text.

By the end of this tutorial you will be able to:

- Work with artistic, shape and frame text.

- Create, edit, and format all types of text.

- Create text-on-a-path.

- Change the shape and fill of text frames.

In this tutorial, you can either work from scratch using a blank drawing (available from the **Start New Drawing** option on the Startup Wizard), or you can work with the poster that we have already partially designed.

 Go to **http://go.serif.com/resources/DPX6** to download the following resource file(s):

🔘 **poster.dpp**

Let's begin...

1. On the **Standard** toolbar, click  **Open**.

2. Locate the **poster.dpp** file and click **Open**.

The poster's graphical background has been placed on a **Background** layer, which has been locked to prevent unintentional modification. A blank, **Text** layer (selected by default) has also been added for displaying your text.

Save now! Click **File > Save As** and choose a new name for your file.

Artistic text

Let's start by adding some artistic text!

To create artistic text:

1. On the **Drawing** toolbar, from the Artistic Text Tool flyout, click the **A** **Artistic Text Tool**.

2. Click on the page to create an insertion point.

3. On the context toolbar, set the size to **120** pt and, from the Font drop-down list, select **Tahoma**.

4. Type the name of your festival.

Next, we'll use the properties of artistic text to make it a little more exciting!

To resize and rotate artistic text:

1. On the **Drawing** toolbar, from the Pointer Tool flyout, click the ↖ **Pointer Tool**.

2. Click on the top-centre handle of the text box and drag upwards. Notice that this stretches the text.

3. Next, click right-centre handle of the text box and drag inwards. Notice that this squashes the text.

4. To rotate the text, hover next to a corner handle. When you see the ↰ cursor, click and drag to rotate the object.

5. Finally, click and drag the ⊞ move button to position the text.

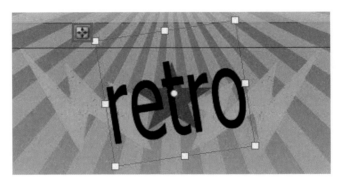

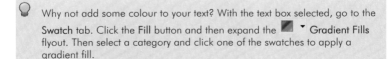

Why not add some colour to your text? With the text box selected, go to the Swatch tab. Click the **Fill** button and then expand the ▪ ▾ **Gradient Fills** flyout. Then select a category and click one of the swatches to apply a gradient fill.

For more on using fills, see *Solid Fills* and *Gradient Fills* on p. 129 and p. 141, respectively.

Don't forget to save your work!

Now let's create a new artistic text object

To create artistic text (alternative method):

1. On the **Drawing** toolbar, click the A **Artistic Text Tool**.

2. Click and drag on the page to set the font size to approximately **30** pt.

3. Type a slogan.

If you're not happy with the way the default font looks, you can easily change it. We'll do this next.

 This method of formatting applies to all types of text.

To select and format existing text:

1. On the **Drawing** toolbar, click the **A** Artistic Text Tool.

2. Click inside the text box next to the first letter, and then drag to highlight all of the text. (You can also press **Ctrl** + **A** or triple click.) The selected text is highlighted blue.

3. On the context toolbar, in the font drop-down list, select **Tahoma**.

4. On the **Swatch** tab, select the **Fill** button and click white. The text formatting is updated.

Don't forget to save your work!

Next we'll show you how to fit text to a curve.

Putting text on a path

Next, we'll fit our text to a curved path. With the text object
selected, on the context toolbar, the <img> ▾ **Preset Text Paths** flyout
offers a range of preset paths (such as the ⌒ **Curved Text - Top
Circle** illustrated below).

However, in this tutorial, we'll show you how to fit a text object to
an existing line. You can fit text to any previously drawn line—we
created a curved line for you, based on the ellipse on the
Background layer.

To put text on a path:

1. On the **Drawing** toolbar, click the 🖰 **Pointer Tool**.

2. Select the text object and then hold down the **Shift** key and
    select the curved line.

3. From the **Tools** menu, select **Fit Text to Curve**.

4. To change the position of the text along the line, ensure that the **A Artistic Text Tool** is selected and click in the text to create an insertion point.

5. Drag the Start (or End) point arrow to move the text so it sits neatly along the hill shape.

6. Finally, to place the text beneath the curve line, drag the alignment handle to the bottom of the bar.

7. Finally, click and drag the move button to position the text.

Search *Fitting text to a path* in DrawPlus Help for more information.

 Don't forget to save your work!

Adding text to shapes

Now let's add some information about our Retro festival using the Quick Rectangles.

To create shape text:

1. On the **Drawing** toolbar, click the ⬉ **Pointer Tool** and select the left hand rectangle.

2. On the **Drawing** toolbar, click the **A** **Artistic Text Tool**. An insertion point begins to flash in the centre of the shape.

3. On the context toolbar, select the **Tahoma** font and set the font size to **36** pt. (You might need to adjust this to suit your text.)

4.   Type the information you wish to display.

Congratulations! You've just created shape text!

 Don't forget to save your work!

> Although a shaped text frame and shape text can look similar on the page, they are treated differently by DrawPlus. To find out more about the differences between shape and frame text, search *Entering text, Editing text* and *Fitting text to frames and shape* in DrawPlus Help.

Using text frames

We'll finish the poster by creating a text frame.

To create a text frame:

1.   On the **Drawing** toolbar, on the A ⁻ Text Frames flyout, click the 🖹 Frame Text Tool.

2. Click and drag to create a text frame.

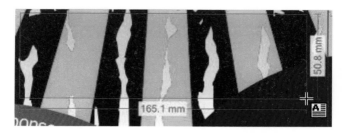

3. On the context toolbar, select the **Tahoma** font and set the size to **20** pt.

4. Type any additional festival information.

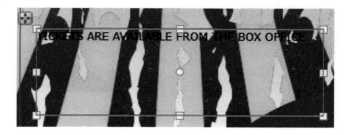

You have created a basic text frame. However, you don't have to stick with a basic rectangle. Let's get creative!

(Optional) To adjust the shape, line and fill of a text frame:

1. On the **Drawing** toolbar, click the ↖ **Pointer Tool**, and select the text frame.

2. On the **Line** tab, increase the line weight to around **2** pt.

3. On the **Swatch** tab, apply a light fill and a dark line.

4. On the **Drawing** toolbar, click the ▷ **Node Tool** and on the context toolbar, from the drop-down list, select **Quick Ellipse**.

5. On the **Drawing** toolbar, click the ⬉ **Pointer Tool** and, from the context toolbar, select ≡ **Centre-align paragraph**.

6. From the **Format** menu, select **Text Flow**.

7. In the **Text Flow** dialog, from the **Vertical alignment** drop-down list, select **Centre** and click **OK**.

The text in your text frame is now centred horizontally and vertically. That's it!

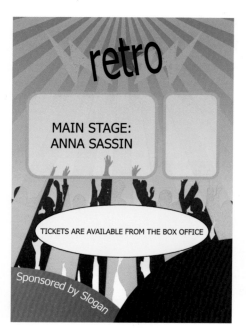

Don't forget to save your work!

There's so much more you can do!

Below are some examples of what else you can do...

Change the text font, size and colour

We updated the font to Abbess, used a variety of text sizes (20, 24 and 36 pt) and varied the colour from black to blue (C=83, M=50, Y=13, K=0).

Customize artistic and frame text

Artistic and frame text can be converted to curves to allow you to customize it further. See the following tutorial, *Customizing Artistic Text*, for more information.

Customizing Artistic Text

🕐 10-15 min ✏️✏️✏️✏️✏️

In this tutorial we'll modify an ordinary font into retro-style text, which would work perfectly for a logo or other branding material.

By the end of this tutorial you will be able to:

- Add text to the page.

- Modify a text style.

- Convert text to curves for further personalization.

- Rotating and repositioning objects.

- Editing the nodes of a curve.

Let's begin...

- In the Startup Wizard, choose **Start New Drawing**, select a page size of your choice and click **OK**.

Adding text

We'll begin by adding text to the page using the Artistic Text Tool.

To create artistic text:

1. On the **Drawing** toolbar, from the Artistic Text Tool flyout, click the **A** Artistic **Text Tool**.

2. Click on the page to create an insertion point.

3. On the context toolbar, set the size to **120** pt and, from the Font drop-down list, select **Tahoma**.

4. Type a word or sentence, e.g. 'retro'.

retro

5. (Optional) With the text still selected, on the **Align** tab, click ⬚ **Centre Horizontally** and ⬚ **Centre Vertically**.

⬚ **Save now!** Click **File** > **Save As** and choose a new name for your file.

Now, we'll modify the text style to bring the text's letters closer together.

Modifying a text style

The Text Style dialog allows you to manipulate your text in a variety of interesting ways. We'll use it to condense our text.

To condense letter spacing:

1. With the text still selected, from the **Format** menu, select **Character**.

    The Text Style dialog opens.

2. In the **Text Style** dialog:

    *   From the left **Character** list, select the **Spacing** option.

    *   From the **Spacing** drop-down list, select **Condensed**.

    *   In the **By** input box, type '12' and click **OK**.

Your text should now resemble the example below.

The position of individual letters can also be modified using the Text Styles dialog. Simply use the Artistic Text Tool to select the letter before accessing the dialog. In the example, we lowered the 'e' by 12 pt.

For more information, search *Editing text* and *Adjusting spacing, justification, and kerning* in DrawPlus Help.

Next, we'll convert the text to curves to allow us to edit each letter individually.

 Don't forget to save your work!

Customizing text

Our text is beginning to look more stylized, but it could do with a bit more work if we want it to really stand out. To allow us to adjust the text in a more radical way, we can convert the text to curves and then individually tweak each letter.

 Once your text is converted to curves you will no longer be able to retype your word(s). It is important to ensure your text is written precisely how you want it, before proceeding. Search *Retyping text* in DrawPlus Help for details.

To convert text to curves:

- With the text still selected, from the **Tools** menu, select **Convert to Curves**.

Now let's start with a simple rotation (or two!)...

To rotate a letter:

1. Click once on the 'e' to select the letter.

2. Position the cursor just outside a corner handle on the bounding box until the ↖↘ rotate cursor displays, then click and drag to rotate the letter anti-clockwise.

3. Click once on the 'o' to select the letter.

4. Repeat step 2 above, rotating the letter clockwise, or for more precise rotating, on the **Transform** tab, set the ↻ rotation angle to **340°**.

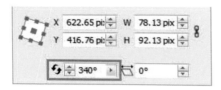

Now let's reposition a few letters...

To move a letter:

•   With the 'o' still selected, click and drag the letter to the left until it is positioned similar to the example below. Holding down the **Shift** key as you drag will restrain the movement to the horizontal.

The text is starting to look good! However, we've not yet taken full advantage of converting the text to curves—editing individual nodes! It sounds complicated, but it isn't—we'll show you next.

 Don't forget to save your work!

Editing nodes

Editing the individual nodes of a letter can help you create some amazing effects. We'll concentrate on some simple tweaks, but feel free to go as radical as you like.

To edit individual nodes:

1. On the **Drawing** toolbar, click the ▷ **Node Tool** and click to select the first 'r'.

   To edit the letter's nodes accurately you may need to zoom in.

2. (Optional) From the **View** menu, click **Selection**.

   Your selected letter should now fill your screen.

3. Click to select the top, right node closest to the 'e'.

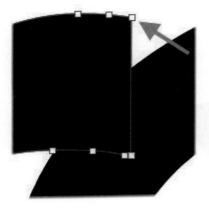

The node will change colour to indicate it is selected and will display handles.

4. Click and drag the selected node until it is positioned within the boundary of the 'e'.

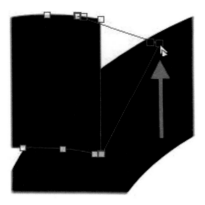

The lines connecting the selected nodes and those either side are too straight—we want them more curved.

5. With the node still selected, from the context toolbar, click ⌂ **Smart Corner.**

6. (Optional) Click and drag the selected node to ensure the top of the 'r' has a smooth arch.

Now we'll look at editing multiply nodes!

To edit multiple nodes:

1. With the 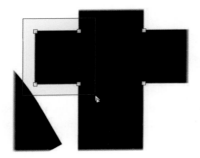 Node Tool, select the letter 't'.

2. Position the cursor just above and to the left of the letter's crossbar and then click and drag a box around the four nodes as shown below.

The nodes will change colour to indicated they are selected.

3. On the context toolbar, click ⚏ Delete Node.

The left side of the crossbar instantly disappears!

That's it! Your stylized text is now finished. You can now print it, export it, or copy it to the Gallery tab to use in other DrawPlus projects.

 Don't forget to save your work!

There's so much more you can do!

Below are some examples of what else you can do...

Apply different colours

Select each letter individually and then apply a fill colour using the **Colour** or **Swatch** tabs. We chose colours from the **Standard CMYK** palette on the **Swatch** tab. For more information, see *Solid Fills* on p. 129.

Merge letters and apply line colour

Use the **Shape Builder Tool** (search *Joining objects* in DrawPlus Help) to join the letters together, set a line weight using the **Line** tab, and then apply a line colour to the resulting object. We chose H=30, S=85, L=50 at a line weight of **2.3** pt.

Adding Spiral Decorations to Text

🕙 10 min ✏️✏️✏️✏️✏️

In this tutorial we'll show you how to add swirls and flourishes to your text to change a basic font into beautiful script. The resulting text would work excellently as a company logo particularly where the logo complements the basic font used on the company's website or other promotional material.

⚠️ This tutorial does not discuss OpenType features (available with some fonts) which allow you to automatically add flourishes to your text as you type. Search *Fonts with OpenType features* in DrawPlus Help for more information.

By the end of this tutorial you will be able to:

- Add text to the page.

- Add flourishes using the Spiral Tool.

- Flip, rotate and move objects.

- Use preset pressure profiles.

Let's begin...

- In the Startup Wizard, choose **Start New Drawing**, select a page size of your choice and click **OK**.

Adding text

We'll begin by adding text to the page using the Artistic Text Tool.

To create artistic text:

1. On the **Drawing** toolbar, from the Artistic Text Tool flyout, click the **A** **Artistic Text Tool**.

2. Click on the page to create an insertion point.

3. On the context toolbar, set the size to 120 pt and, from the font drop-down list, select **Times New Roman**.

4. Type a word or sentence, e.g. 'Vines'.

Vines

5. (Optional) With the text still selected, on the **Align** tab, click 🖫 **Centre Horizontally** and 🗐 **Centre Vertically**.

Now let's update the text with a few flourishes!

🖫 Don't forget to save your work!

Adding spiral flourishes

The Spiral Tool allows you to quickly and easily add flourishes to any text. Provided the spiral lines are the same colour as the text's line and fill, they'll blend in perfectly. We're going to walk you through adding some flourishes to the 'V'.

To add a spiral:

1. On the **Drawing** toolbar, from the Pen Tool flyout, click the  Spiral Tool.

2. Position the spiral cursor at the position where you want the centre of the spiral to be.

3. Hold down the mouse button and drag outward to draw and position the end of your spiral.

4. Release the mouse button when you are happy with the spiral. The spiral is added to your page with its nodes displayed.

You can adjust the spiral as it is being drawn, using the arrow keys on the keyboard—we'll look at this next.

To adjust a spiral during creation:

1. With the **Spiral Tool** still selected, repeat steps 2 and 3 as before, this time positioning the spiral's centre to the left of the 'V'.

2. With the mouse button held down, use the left or right arrow keys to adjust the length of the spiral.

We used the right arrow key to create a lazy spiral with few turns.

We'll add more spirals to our text, but before doing so, let's look at several ways in which you can edit the spirals once they are on your page...

 Don't forget to save your work!

Editing spirals

We'll look at several ways you can edit your spiral once it has been created. For this, we created a third spiral which we want to reposition so that it appears to extend from the V's top serif.

To rearrange a spiral:

1. On the **Drawing** toolbar, from the Pointer Tool flyout, click the  Pointer Tool.

2. Click to select the spiral and then, on the **Standard** toolbar, click ⚠ **Flip Horizontal**.

> Alternatively, you can flip a spiral on creation by pressing the X key while dragging using the Spiral Tool. Search *Drawing spirals* in DrawPlus Help for more information on creating spirals and using modifier keys.

3. On the **Transform** tab, set the ↻ rotation angle so the spiral will extend neatly from the V's serif. We set ours to **75°**.

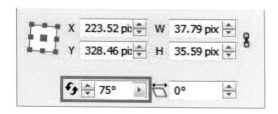

4.   Click and drag the spiral's 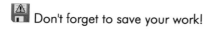 move button to position the spiral do it appears to extend from the V's serif.

The spirals currently appear too linear in thickness. However, we want the spirals to resemble natural vines (to fit with the word 'Vines'). We can do this using preset pressure profiles!

Don't forget to save your work!

To add a preset pressure profile:

•   With the spiral selected, on the **Pressure** tab, from the preset profiles drop-down list, select the descending linear gradient.

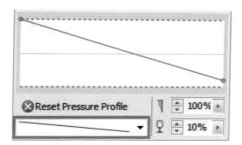

The spiral will now appear thinner at the centre and thicker at the end.

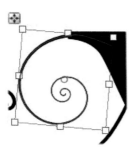

 Selecting an ascending linear gradient will result in a spiral which appears thicker at the centre and thinner at the end.

To complete the illusion that the spiral is growing from the V's serif, we need to increase the thickness of the line.

To increase line weight:

- With the spiral selected, on the **Line** tab, drag the weight slider to set the thickness to **2.5 pt**.

The first letter is now complete!

🖫 Don't forget to save your work!

Completing the design

Now you have the hang of adding spirals and editing them, why not add spirals to the remaining text letters to complete your design.

That's it! Your stylized text is now finished.

🖫 Don't forget to save your work!

There's so much more you can do!

Below are some examples of what else you can do...

Convert text to curves for a more customized look

You can reposition and edit the nodes of individual letters once they have been converted to curves. This allows for a much more stylized and customized look.

See *Customizing Artistic Text* (p. 195) for more information.

Create complementary spirals and swirls

The Spiral Tool can be used to create beautiful natural spiral designs. Experiment and see what you can create!

Creative Showcase

DrawPlus X6 provides many preset brushes and professionally designed stencils, gallery content, and graphic styles to help you create stunning compositions and graphical art. Sample files are also included for inspiration!

Brushes

DrawPlus provides a large collection of creative brushes for you to get creative with. These brushes are stored in categories in the **Brushes** tab, and include **Draw**, **Effects**, **Grunge**, **Paint** and **Spray**.

To apply a brush stroke:

1.   On the **Drawing** toolbar, click the 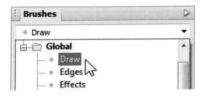 **Brush Tool**.

2.   On the **Brushes** tab, from the category drop-down list, select a category.

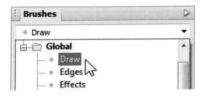

The category's gallery is displayed in the tab.

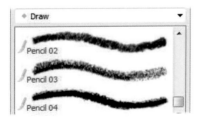

3.   Click to select a preset brush from the gallery and then click and drag across your page to paint your lines.

We'll showcase the **Draw** (as selected above), **Paint** and **Spray** categories next.

Draw

Paint

Spray

Stencils

Stencils open up a whole world of creative opportunities and are fun and simple to use.

To use stencils to draw and design:

1. On the **Stencils** tab, from the category drop-down list, select a category to display its gallery in the tab.

2. Click and drag a thumbnail from the gallery onto the page.

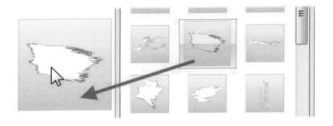

3. On the **Drawing** toolbar, click the ✐ **Brush Tool** and then select a brush type from the **Brushes** tab (as described on p. 217).

4. Paint over the stencil with your brush strokes.

5. On the **Drawing** toolbar, click the ➤ **Pointer Tool**, and then click to select the stencil and, on the Stencil context toolbar, click ⬚ **Lift Stencil**.

   Search *Using stencils* in DrawPlus Help for more information.

We'll showcase the **Artistic** (as selected above) and **Shapes** categories next.

Artistic

Shapes I

Shapes II

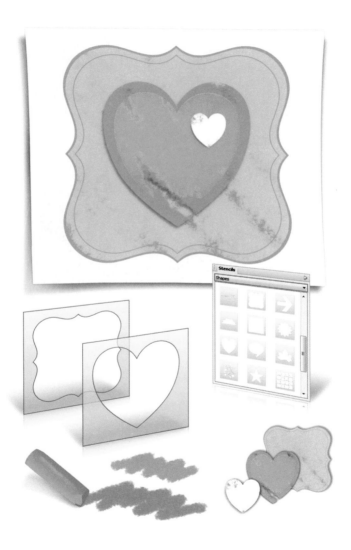

Gallery Content

The DrawPlus **Gallery** tab provides a wealth of resources to help you create a multitude of different documents, charts, and drawings.

The Gallery (p. 3) tutorial shows you how to add, use and modify Gallery shapes and objects, so we'll not go into details here.

Instead we'll showcase the **ShapeArt** > **Embossed Shapes** and **ClipArt** > **Easter** sub-categories next.

ShapeArt > Embossed Shapes

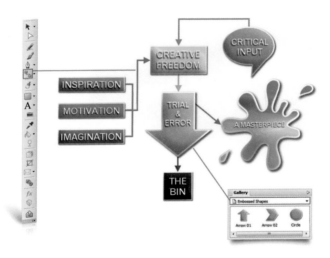

ClipArt > Easter

Graphic Styles

The **Styles** tab provides you with pre-designed graphic styles which you can apply to any object on your page.

To apply a graphic style to objects:

1. Select an object on your page.

2. On the **Styles** tab, from the category drop-down list, select a category.

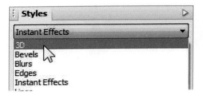

The category's gallery is displayed in the tab.

3. Click a thumbnail to instantly apply it to the selected object.

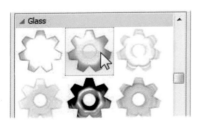

Search *Using graphic styles* in DrawPlus Help for more information.

We'll showcase the **3D** and **Instant Effects** categories next.

3D and Instant Effects

Styles

3D

Mixed

Instant Effects

Glass

Bevel & Emboss

Feather Edge

3D Effect

Glass Effect

Samples

DrawPlus is installed with sample drawings which show how the program can be used to create ready-to-print drawings and stunning digital art, as well as for designing logos and marketing material, and produce animations. These sample files, categoroized as **Featured Users**, **Art**, **Illustration**, **Print**, **Paper Crafts**, **Stopframe Animation**, and **Keyframe Animation**, are available directly from the **Startup Wizard**.

To open a DrawPlus sample file:

1. From the **Startup Wizard**, in the **View** section, click **Sample Designs**.

2. In the **Choose a Sample** dialog:

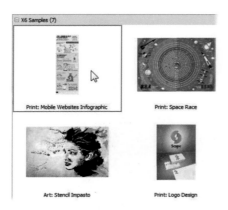

-   Click to select a thumbnail.

-   Click **OK**.

We'll showcase a range of the samples next.